Lost, Stolen or Strayed

Lost, Stolen or Strayed

The Story of the Battersea Dogs' Home

Gloria Cottesloe

Arthur Barker Limited
5 Winsley Street London W1

For John, but also for the dogs

SBN 0 213 00414 3

Printed in Great Britain by
Willmer Brothers Limited, Birkenhead

Contents

Acknowledgements

The picture of HRH Princess Alice with the dog thought to be the one her father, Prince Leopold, took from the Home, together with other material from the Royal Archives, is published by gracious permission of Her Majesty the Queen.

For permission to reproduce the other illustrations, the author and publishers are indebted to Freddie Reed of the *Daily Mirror*, the *Radio Times* Hulton Picture Library, the Royal Geographical Society, and the *Daily Express*.

Illustrations

Author's Note

I cannot publish this book without saying how indebted I am to Mr Jack Tyler for the meticulous and loving work he has carried out in sifting and annotating the mass of material that exists at the Dogs' Home. Without his work, the book could never have been written.

I would like to take the opportunity of thanking Lt Commander Knight and his staff at Battersea, not only for the help they have given to me personally, but also for the splendid work they are carrying out daily.

I am extremely grateful to HRH Princess Alice, Countess of Athlone for her help in what may have proved to be the correct identification of the dog that Prince Leopold took from the Home in 1883.

I have received help from many quarters, and am particularly grateful to Mr Robert Mackworth-Young, the Librarian at Windsor, who went to an infinite amount of trouble to help me with the material from the Royal Archives. I must say a special word of thanks to Mr Freddie Reed of the *Daily Mirror* who took photographs for the book, including the cover which the Picture Editor of the *Daily Mirror* has generously allowed to be used without charge as a donation to the Home. I am also grateful to the Marquess of Townshend, to the Borough Librarian of the Wandsworth Public Libraries, to Mr E. A. Willats, the Reference Librarian at the Islington Libraries, and to Mrs Dorothy Owen, the Ely Diocesan Archivist. I would like to thank Dr Terence Armstrong, Deputy Director of the Scott Antarctic Institute at Cambridge, and Mr Walter How, one of the surviving members of Shackleton's 1914 Expedition, for their help. Mr T. Richardson of the RSPCA and the Secretary of the British Union for the Abolition of Vivisection provided most useful material.

Finally, my especial thanks are due to Miss Judith Larkin who looked after my family, and Miss Christina Cleathero who typed the manuscript.

I

The Early Beginnings

Dogs have been the friends of man since the time of Mesolithic man (10,000 BC). Huntsmen and dogs in the Magdalenian frescoes of Spain have been identified as such and ascribed to that era. Through the ages, bones have been unearthed amid piles of debris outside human habitations bearing marks that the archaeologists say could only have been made by the teeth of dogs, thus showing that dogs were in fact always there, sharing man's hearth, his home and his food.

Once accepted by man, the dog became his slave and his defender. It barked to give warning and to drive off intruders, and it was not long before man realized the full value of such a friend, workmate and companion. Soon the dog was carrying burdens, dragging primitive sledges, and learning the art of disciplined hunting. It became the guardian of the pasture and of the home, but most important of all for our story is the fact that man and dog became dependent on each other, forging not only bonds of utility, but also the bonds of mutual devotion.

Prehistoric man did not show his dog in his paintings side by side with bison, boar and reindeer, for the dog was his friend, not his prey. Man had never needed to fight dog nor to subjugate it by force, or we would have found proofs of this in the rock drawings he made of his battles. There must have been a pattern of coexistence that led to complete domestication of the animal.

If we study the work of artists throughout the ages there

is much that we can learn, not only of their art, but also of day to day life at the time they lived. Prominent among the work of artists all over the world from the earliest times is the dog; big dogs, little dogs, lap dogs, hunting dogs – they sleep at the feet of warriors, they adorn the silken laps of queens, they leap at the throats of their prey, and they share the feasts of festivity throughout the ages. Dogs are portrayed in oil paintings, charcoal drawings, in marble, bronze and in precious stones. They appear on early seals, later on coins, and later still they adorn inn signs and postage stamps. No historical scene of domestic life seemed to be complete without its attendant dog, gnawing a bone under the table or enjoying a skirmish with a cat in the corner. Dogs had demanded a place in man's life, and that is what they have had ever since.

However, what about the other side of the canine picture? There was another side, and one that was very different from that idealized by artists. Not all dogs were destined to grace the houses of the rich, nor even the dwellings of the poor, and this is how the story of the Dogs' Home at Battersea came about.

It begins not as you would expect, south of the river Thames, but in the north London borough of Holloway in 1860, half-a-dozen years after the women's prison was built, when the district was still a middle-class residential suburb, virtually a village on the edge of that great city, the capital of the British Empire.

London was growing at the rate of more than two thousand houses each year, with a population expanding to fill them, not only through the enormously large Victorian families that prevailed at that time amongst both rich and poor – to the rich the family was all-sacred; the poor had little alternative – but by a constant flow of immigrants from Ireland and from Scotland who came to escape poverty and to seek their fortunes. The total population of England and Wales increased by about five million in the twenty years between 1851 and 1871, and a large proportion of this number made their way

2

to London, that city where the streets were traditionally paved with gold.

Those immigrants must have been quickly and sadly disillusioned, for instead of gold they found mud. It was not the swinging London of a hundred years later, but stinking London, a city of open drains and of disease; a city where in a court twenty-two feet wide with a common sewer running down the middle, there dwelt nearly a thousand people in twenty-six three-storeyed houses. It was small wonder that febrile influenza, typhoid and cholera took their yearly toll.

The twin enemies of filth and disease began to retreat with the establishment of the Parliamentary Sewer Commissioners in the middle of the century. They laid down over fifty miles of underground arterial drainage and pumped out millions of cubic feet of stinking sludge. They were backed up in their work by the further establishment in 1855 of the Metropolitan Board of Works, the forerunner of the London County Council and later of the GLC. This body, however, only existed until 1888, by which time it was known as 'the Board of Perks', so many of its members having their own profitable axes to grind.

Those reputedly gold-paved streets were in fact solid with Victorian citizens going about their business amid the noise and clamour of a type of traffic that would defeat our police today.

Horse-drawn vehicles vied with pedestrians, who in their turn had to skip to avoid ankle-deep horse dung and the slime that putrified in the gutters. On the one side they were in danger of going under the wheels of buses, hearses, and wagons, and on the other they were in danger of being trampled by the hooves of reluctant cattle or bewildered sheep being driven on their way to Smithfield for slaughter.

Pandemonium reigned and the roads were solidly blocked by this phalanx of ill-assorted traffic. At the sides of the roads stood the beggars exhibiting their sores and holding out their tins. In and out of the crowds darted the light-fingered street

3

urchins trying to make a dishonest living. Street vendors cried their wares on the pavements' edges, knocked sideways by the sharp corners of the sandwich boards that weighed down their shambling bearers.

Horses neighed, cows mooed, sheep bleated and men shouted, while amid this wilderness of filth ran an army of hungry, disease-ridden dogs, scavenging in the piles of ordure that lay at every street corner, savagely fighting each other for a dirty piece of bread or for a broken bit of bone. These animals were covered with sores, alive with vermin, homeless, unloved, unlovable.

Yet it was one of this starving horde of hungry animals that was to bring about a change in the destiny of the stray dog and help to revolutionize the whole picture of the London scene.

We shall never know what this dog looked like, nor even what eventually happened to it, for no records remain. What we do know is that a small dog was found starving in the gutter by a middle-aged widow in Islington. Horrified by its condition, she took it into her house.

This was during a summer's afternoon in 1860. Later that same afternoon the good samaritan, whose name was Mrs Major, was visited by a friend, another middle-aged lady called Mrs Tealby.

No doubt the visitor was shown into the parlour by a little beribboned parlourmaid, but a moment or two later, Mrs Major came excitedly into the room. A little hot and dishevelled with tendrils of hair escaping from their pins, Mrs Major told her friend that before they had a cup of tea there was something she wanted to show her.

Leading the way out of the parlour into the narrow hall again, she went down the steep stairs that led to the kitchen and the servants' quarters, normally an area seldom penetrated by a mistress, and certainly never by a guest. Mrs Tealby, mystified, followed closely and they went into what would have been a typical mid-Victorian kitchen, dominated by the enormous black-leaded range, which even at the height of summer had to kept alight so that the meals could be cooked and the water heated for domestic use.

There beside the fire was a pathetic sight, a small dog lying stretched out on a piece of old blanket, hardly seeming to be alive, its breathing swift and shallow.

There must have been something exceptional about this little waif from the London streets; maybe it wagged its tail feebly, or perhaps it tried to struggle to its feet to welcome the visitors, or to lick Mrs Tealby's hand as she bent to stroke it. Anyway, as Mrs Tealby looked down at this little animal, her heart went out, and the germ of an idea came to her mind, an idea that led to the foundation of an institution that has provided help and succour for more than two and a quarter million stray dogs.

We can guess that Mrs Major was kind and soft hearted, for very soon that little dog was joined by several others, and Mrs Tealby readily helped her to nurse them back to health – probably a health that the poor creatures had never before known, being puppies of the cruel streets and not well-nurtured pets from comfortable homes. What we know without a doubt is that Mrs Tealby must have been of the stuff that in later years the suffragettes were made, reflecting the determination of her contemporary Florence Nightingale. She was evidently a woman of drive and purpose who needed a cause for which to fight. The fact that Mrs Tealby, who was certainly the leading light in the partnership, was able to enthuse her friend, Mrs Major, to the extent that she did, and the fact that these two women resolutely started to do something about the situation that they found, must have been one of the ripples on the surface that indicated the beginning of the wave of humanitarianism that started in the middle of the last century, expanding and spreading, until now the world is flooded with societies manned by people who wish to improve the lot of others, whether those others be animal or human.

With quiet determination, Mrs Tealby set about her task. First she enlisted the help of her brother, a retired clergyman called Edward Bates with whom she had lived in a rented house in Victoria Road since the break-up of her marriage. It was essential that they should have the aid of a man at that stage, and who better than Edward Bates who had been educated at Uppingham and Clare College, Cambridge? He had held livings in Northamptonshire and knew many influential people.

Mrs Tealby visited all her friends and wrote endless letters, appealing for money and support, persuading her friends to do the same. The result of these labours was an initial subscription list that contained 172 names of people from as far apart as Cumberland, Aberystwyth and Hamilton in Ireland, and which ranged from such names as those of His Imperial Highness, the Prince Louis Lucien Bonaparte, nephew of Napoleon, and the Dowager Countess of Essex, down to Puff, a pet, and 'Pussy' Davidson.

Mrs Tealby soon discovered that there were thousands of poor wretched dogs roaming the London streets, born only to live a life of starvation and terror, literally hounded from place to place, pelted with refuse and cruelly tormented. Their pathetic condition excited little pity and no compassion in the minds of those who saw them, and the few morsels of food that came their way had to be fought for when they possessed the strength, and when that strength was lacking, all that was left for them was just to lie down quietly in some corner and die.

This undoubtedly was exactly what Mrs Major's first little dog was doing when she came across him – lying down to die. However, just five months after that little dog had been brought to the kitchen in Canonbury Square, thanks to the energetic drive of Mrs Tealby, a committee meeting was held in November at the Pall Mall offices of the Royal Society for the Prevention of Cruelty to Animals.

In the chair of this meeting was Lord Raynham, Member of Parliament for Tamworth, Warwickshire and heir to the Marquess of Townshend. Lord Raynham was well known for his love of animals and stories are told in his family of his keen interest in animal welfare and how he would buy them from street traders, birds and pet shops and take them back to his home, Raynham Hall in Norfolk. Known as 'the Good Marquess', an inscription on the back of a Spy cartoon refers to him as the beggar's friend. Even so, it is surprising that a middle-aged woman living in Holloway should have persuaded an undoubted member of the aristocracy to take such a large part in the affairs of what up to then was still only an ideal and not an established fact. Social strata were severely separated by unbridgeable gulfs, and a middle-class woman, especially from a London suburb, was as likely to sit down to tea with a navvy as to find herself on calling terms with a marquis – unless of course she happened to be a particularly beautiful chorus girl.

At that historic November meeting the following resolutions were proposed by the Chairman and adopted unanimously:

1 That an Institution be now established for the care of lost and starving dogs.

2 That the following be the rules of the Institution:
   a That the name of the Institution be 'The Home for Lost and Starving Dogs'.
   b That an annual subscriber of five shillings or a donor of five pounds be a Governor of the Institution.
   c That the Institution be under the Management of a Treasurer, Honorary Secretary, and a Committee.
   d That there be an Annual General Meeting of the Governors to receive a Report from the Committee of the proceedings of the Society and a Financial Statement for the past year, and to elect the Committee and Honorary Officers for the ensuing year.
   e That a Special General Meeting may be summoned on the requisition to the Honorary Secretary of any ten Governors, not less than fourteen days from the receipt of the requisition, the object of the Meeting being stated in the circular to the Governors.

3   That Captain Jesse be Treasurer; the Rev. Edward Bates, MA, the Honorary Secretary, and the following ladies and gentlemen be Members of the Committee:

Rev. Edw. Bates, MA   Mrs Ratcliffe Chambers
Mrs Hambleton   Mrs Jesse
Mrs Liveing   Mrs Major
Miss Morgan   Mrs Tealby
          William Chambers, Esq.

Today the articles of association provide that:

5   Any person in sympathy with the aims of the Association who shall give to the Association in one amount a sum of money not less than £5 shall, on such payment, become qualified to be a Life Member of the Association.

6   Every person in sympathy with the aims of the Association who shall have paid a sum of five shillings and upwards to the funds of the Association shall be qualified to be a member of the Association.

9   Every Member of the Association (other than a Life Member) shall pay an annual subscription to the funds of the Association of at least five shillings.

These figures do not reflect the rise in the cost of living or the fall in the value of the pound since that historic meeting one hundred and eleven years ago, when a small institution was founded in a backyard by two or three enthusiasts which was destined to grow, thrive and to become known the world over.

2

The Struggle for Establishment

By the time of that first meeting in November, 1860, a dog's home of sorts had in fact already been started six weeks earlier in Holloway, not far from the street where Mrs Major had found the first starving dog, and close to where Mrs Tealby lived.

It was sited in a mews in Hollingsworth Street, which lies between the Caledonian and Holloway Roads, and was reached through a carriage-way between two rows of houses. The stables that ran behind the rows of houses were converted into kennels, and the stableyard in front of them into a run for the dogs. A nearby house was rented for a resident keeper.

A contemporary description of a dog's entry into the home gives us a good picture of what happened when an animal arrived there.

A man is engaged to take charge of the animals, to answer questions of applicants who bring dogs or claim them, and to keep the necessary record of in-comers and out-goers. When a dog becomes a member of this happy family, he is named, and this name, and his breed (if ascertainable) are entered in a book under a particular number. A tin ticket with a corresponding number is then hung round his neck, and he is provided with a place in a certain trough, basket, box, cage, or tub, according to his temper and his bodily health.

This procedure has hardly changed to this day, though with anything up to twenty thousand dogs entering the

Home each year, the practice of naming had to cease many years ago. Back in 1860 the dogs were kept for at least fourteen days before being sold or otherwise disposed of. Being otherwise disposed of was a necessary euphemism to enable the soft-hearted ladies to forget that a drop of prussic acid was the only way of dealing with the overwhelming problem. The ladies could hardly bring themselves to agree to the destruction of any of their charges, and a rule that had started as 'Any dog brought to the Home and not identified and claimed within fourteen days from the time of admission will, by order of the Committee, be sold to pay expenses, or otherwise disposed of' was very soon modified to 'That the number of dogs that have been in the Home longer than fourteen days be kept down as nearly as possible to forty'.

The Committee were very fortunate in their first servant, James Pavitt. He came to them at the start and remained in the service of the Home until his death in 1883. In 1874 his daughter, Rosa, joined the staff as a clerk, and she later married her father's assistant, George Tagg, who was eventually to succeed his father-in-law as head keeper. The Pavitts set the pattern of long service, dedication and devotion to duty that has been extraordinarily marked in the staff right through the history of the Dogs' Home.

By and large, the establishment of such a home was greeted by the Press with jeering mockery. Sentiment was out of keeping with the times, and many leading newspapers joined in the general calumny and ridicule, which must have served to double the work of the small Committee as they struggled to raise the money that they needed to make their dreams take form.

However in 1859, the year before our story begins, Charles Dickens, who was described by his contemporaries as not so much a man as an institution, had started a new venture. This was a journal to be called *All the Year Round,* designed to succeed his successful twopenny weekly, *Household Harmony. All the Year Round* started with the serialization of *A Tale of Two Cities,* followed by *Great Expectations* and *Our Mutual Friend.* A journalist refreshingly lacking in spurious artistic ideals, but burning with an intense desire for the sympathy of his readers, Charles Dickens plunged into this new venture with such vigour, that within the first three months his new journal had earned enough to pay him five per cent interest on all the money he had advanced out of his own pocket for its establishment, still leaving him with £500 in the bank.

On Saturday, 2 August 1862 *All the Year Round* published its one hundred and seventy-first issue, and in it was an article entitled *Two Dog-Shows* which set out to compare a visit to a prize Dog Show at the Islington Hall, followed by a visit to a dog show of a very different sort a mile away in Holloway.

More than a century later, this article expresses so exactly the sentiments one would feel on following a visit to Cruft's Dog Show at Olympia by another immediately afterwards to the Dogs' Home at Battersea, only a mile or two away across the river, that one is tempted to think that it was only written last year, last month, last week. It describes perfectly the stance of the successful, well-fed and valuable dogs, and compares their good fortune with the woeful misery of the abandoned, ever buoyed up by their good humour and the optimism that does not let them down, whoever else has done so.

It has been said that every individual member of the human race bears in his outward form a resemblance to some animal; and I really believe that (you, the reader, and I, the writer of these words, excepted) this is very generally the case. Everybody surely can with ease point out among his friends some who resemble owls, hawks, giraffes, kangaroos, terriers, goats, monkeys. Do we not all know people who are like sheep, pigs, cats, or parrots; the last being, especially in military neighbourhoods, a very common type indeed? Let any one pay a visit to the Zoological Gardens with this theory of resemblances in his mind, and see how continually he will be reminded of his friends.

But what is more remarkable is, that there is one single tribe of animals, and that the most mixed up with man of all, whose different members recall to us constantly different types of humanity. It is impossible to see a large collection of dogs together without being continually reminded of the countenances of people you have met or known; of their countenances, and of their ways.

In that great canine competition which drew crowds, some week or two ago, to Islington, there were furnished many wonderful opportunities for moralising on humanity. It was difficult to keep the fancy within bounds. With regard to the prize dogs for instance (to plunge into the subject at once), was there not something of human malice and disappointment about the look of the unsuccessful competitors? Was there not a tendency in these last to turn their backs upon the winners, and to assume an indifference which they did not feel? There was a certain prize retriever, and a more beautiful animal never wagged tail. To see that creature sitting up and looking with an air of surprise towards the direction in which some other (and probably unsuccessful) dogs were making an immense noise with discontented growlings and barkings— to see his calm expression and utter want of sympathy—was a great sight, and the curled-up disgust of the other retriever who had failed, and whose position was next to that of the prize dog, was even a greater sight. On the whole, the winning dogs carried their honours with calmness, and with the exception of the prize King Charles, the bearing of whose nose was a thought arrogant, sustained their triumph with modesty and forbearance. It is not difficult to occupy the first place becomingly. The winners of such high prizes can afford to be quiet and unassuming. But to feel that you can retrieve better than the prize retriever, that you can hang on to a bull's nose better than the prize bull-dog, that you can make yourself generally disagreeable better than the prize lap-dog, is a worrying thought for the second class competitor, and is apt to make him curl himself up and snap and render himself in a variety of ways hugely unpopular. . . .

The beauty of one dog, the ugliness of another, and most of all the utmost development of the individual peculiarities of the species to which they belonged would seem to have been the causes operating with the judges. . . . Meanwhile, to be bandy, blear-eyed, pink-nosed, blotchy, under-hung and utterly disreputable, is the bull-dog's proudest boast. The bloodhound's skin should hang in ghastly folds about his throat and jaws, with a dewlap like a bull. The King Charles's spaniel wears a fringe upon his legs like a sailor's trousers, and has a nose turned up so abruptly that you could hang your hat upon it if it were not so desperately short. The prize terrier wins because he weighs two pounds and three-quarters, and the boar-hound wins because he would (to look at him) turn the balance with a Shetland pony on the other scale. Truly, the qualifications of dogs are numerous, and very various their claims on our admiration. We give a medal to a Cuban hound for tearing down a fugitive slave, and to an Italian greyhound for wearing a paletot[1] and trembling from head to foot (I saw him) when a fly enters his cage. . . .

Great monster boar-hound, alone worth a moderate journey to get a sight of; sweet-faced muff from St Bernard, whose small intellect is what might be expected of a race living on the top of a mountain with only monks for company; small shadow-faced Maltese terrier; supple fox-hound; beloved pug; detested greyhound of Italy; otter-hounds that look like north country game-keepers—each and all I bid you farewell and proceed yet a little further on my way through the suburbs of North London.

Curiously enough, within a mile of that great dog-show at Islington there existed, and exists still, another dog-show of a very different kind, and forming as complete a contrast to the first as can well be imagined. As you enter the enclosure of this other dog-show, which you approach by certain small thoroughfares of the Holloway district, you find yourself in a queer region, which looks, at first, like a combination of playground and mews. The playground is enclosed on three sides by walls, and on the fourth by a screen of iron cage-work. As soon as you come within sight of this cage some twenty or thirty dogs of every conceivable and inconceivable breed, rush towards the bars, and, flattening their poor snouts against the wires, ask in their own peculiar and most forcible language whether you are their master come at last to claim them?

For this second dog-show is nothing more nor less than the show of the Lost Dogs of the Metropolis—the poor vagrant homeless curs that one sees looking out for a dinner in the gutter, or curled up in a doorway taking refuge from their troubles in sleep. To rescue these miserable animals from slow starvation, to provide an asylum where, if it is of the slightest use, they can be restored with food, and kept till a situation can be found for them; or where

[1] A loose cloak

the utterly useless and diseased cur can be in an instant put out of his misery with a dose of prussic acid—to effect these objects, and also to provide a means of restoring lost dogs to their owners, a society has actually be formed and has worked for some year and a half with very tolerable success. . . .

At the Islington dog-show all was prosperity. Here, all is adversity. There, the exhibited animals were highly valued, and had all their lives been well fed, well housed, carefully watched. Here, for the most part, the poor things had been half-starved and houseless, while as to careful watching, there was plenty of that in one sense, the vigilant householder having watched most carefully his entrance gate to keep such intruders out. At Islington there were dogs estimated by their owners at hundreds of pounds. Here there are animals that are, only from a humane point of view, worth the drop of prussic acid which puts them out of their misery. . . .

Was it purely an over-indulged fancy that made me discern a great moral difference between the dogs at the Islington Show and those at the Refuge in Holloway?

I must confess that it did appear to me that there was in those most prosperous dogs at the 'show', a slight occasional tendency to 'give themselves airs'. They seemed to regard themselves as public characters who really could not be bored by introductions to private individuals. When these last addressed them, by name too, and in that most conciliatory falsetto which should find its way to a well-conditioned dog's inmost heart, it was too often the case that such advances were received with total indifference, and even in some cases, I regret to say, with a snap. As to any feeling for, or interest in, each other, the prosperous dogs were utterly devoid of both.

Among the unappreciated and lost dogs of Holloway, on the other hand, there seemed a sort of fellowship of misery, while their urbane and sociable qualities were perfectly irresistible. They were not conspicuous in the matter of breed, it must be owned. A tolerable Newfoundland dog, a deer-hound of some pretensions, a setter, and one or two decent terriers were among the company; but for the most part the architecture of these canine vagrants was decidedly of the composite order. That particular member of the dog tribe with whom the reader is so well acquainted and who represents the great and important family of the mongrels

14

was there in all his—absence of—glory. Poor beast, with his long tail left, not to please Sir Edwin Landseer, but because nobody thought it worth while to cut it, with his notched pendant ears, with his heavy paws, his ignoble countenance and servile smile of conciliation, snuffing hither and thither, running to and fro, undecided, uncared for, not wanted, timid, supplicatory—there he was, the embodiment of everything that is pitiful, the same poor pattering wretch who follows you along the deserted streets at night, and whose eyes haunt you as you lie in bed after you have locked him out of your house.

To befriend this poor unhappy animal a certain band of humanely-disposed persons has established this Holloway asylum, and a system has been got to work which has actually since October 1860 rescued at least a thousand lost or homeless dogs from starvation.... It is the kind of institution which a very sensitive person who has suffered acutely from witnessing the misery of a starving animal would wish for, without imagining for a moment that it could ever seriously exist.

It *does* seriously exist, though. An institution in this practical country founded on a sentiment. The dogs are, for the most part, of little or no worth. I don't think the Duke of Beaufort[1] would have much to say to the beagle I saw sniffing about in the enclosure and I imagine that the stout man who owned the smaller terriers at the show would have had little to say to the black-and-tan specimens which mustered strong in numbers, but weak in claims to admiration, in the shut-up house.... The 'Home' is a very small establishment, with nothing imposing about it—nothing that suggests expense or luxury. I think it is rather hard to laugh this humane effort to scorn. If people really think it wrong to spend a very, very little money on that poor cur whose face I frankly own often haunts my memory, after I have hardened myself successfully against him—if people really do consider it an injustice to the poor, to give to this particular institution, let them leave it to its fate; but I think it is somewhat hard that they should turn the whole scheme into ridicule, or assail it with open ferocity as a dangerous competitor, with other enterprises for public favour.... At all events, and whether the sentiment be wholesome or morbid, it is worthy of record that such a place exists; an extraordinary

[1] This would be the 8th Duke, grandfather of the present Duke of Beaufort, who has been President of the Home since 1943.

monument of the remarkable affection with which English people regard the race of dogs; an evidence of that hidden fund of feeling which survives in some hearts even the rough ordeal of London life in the nineteenth century.

This article, if not penned by the great author and journalist himself, appeared under his benevolent auspices, and coming as it did when Press criticism of the Dogs' Home was at its height, it provided a resounding defence for the struggling little Home for Lost and Starving Dogs at Holloway.

Contemporary accounts show Charles Dickens as being regarded almost as a demi-god, his work being viewed by what were then known as 'the lower orders' as a revelation of a new world and one far better than their own, which was only too often poor, lonely and sordid. To us today, Charles Dickens appears more in the role of the man who drew back the velvet curtain to give the rich of his time a glimpse of the squalor that lay hidden behind. What he gave to us today is as clear and vivid a picture of Victorian London as we could possibly have. Charles Dickens himself knew better than anyone how the poor had to live, for had he not had the same struggles? Had he not himself been poor, degraded, self-pitying? The difference between him and the others though was that he had been consumed and fired by ambition, an ambition that was backed by pride, sensitivity and a boundless talent. So where others floundered, Charles Dickens swam on to fame and fortune. From being a waif in the slums of London, he was to dine with princes.

Mrs Tealby herself had taken no notice of the oppressive opposition she was receiving, and it is possible that the criticism she had to endure may have served to increase the intensity of her determination to succeed. Benefactors were hunted down, all subscriptions, however small, were welcome, many of these being received in a box specially designed and made for the purpose by Carlton MacCarthy. This took the form of a begging dog, staff in paw, an upturned hat at its feet ready to receive the offerings. Before long a series of bazaars, sales of work and concerts were being given all over London in aid of the Home.

A newspaper article in 1863 sang a very different song from those heard hitherto: 'This novel but useful charity is now patronised by many titled, wealthy and eminent individuals.'

The cause had been taken up in the Mayfair drawing-rooms and the small back-street home for lost and starving dogs was carried on to what was a new and evermore to be respected level.

3

The Move to Battersea

In 1865, just as the Dogs' Home was really becoming established and more widely known and respected, by one of those cruel strokes of fate that are so difficult to understand, Mrs Mary Tealby, whose name appears in every annual report of the Home as the 'Foundress and Unwearied Benefactress of this Institution', died from cancer after a long and painful illness, just one day after her beloved Dogs' Home had celebrated its fifth anniversary.

One is happy to know that before she died she could clearly see that the institution she had founded was obviously destined to survive and prosper.

In the year of her death an appeal was made by the Home for money to establish receiving houses for dogs to be situated in various parts of London, for although one or two abortive attempts had been made to do this, up to then nothing specific had been arranged. Three such places were eventually established, one at Bowling Street in Westminster, another in Arthur Street off the King's Road, Chelsea, and the third in Southampton Street, Bethnal Green. At these agencies dogs were received from anyone who cared to bring them in, but two years later, in 1867, an act of Parliament was passed empowering the police and the police alone to deal with stray dogs. The result of this act was that the police stations throughout the metropolis became receiving houses, and a year later, overwhelmed, the police issued a regulation to the effect that all dogs picked up as strays would be destroyed.

The Committee were desperate, and would have been quite willing to defy the police if necessary and go on collecting dogs themselves. However, matters did not reach this degree of urgency, for after the Rev. G. T. Driffield, a distant cousin of Lord Townshend's, and Mr James Johnson, who had been appointed Superintendent of the Home in 1865, had been to see Sir Richard Mayne, the Chief Commissioner of Metropolitan Police, arrangements were made for dogs to be delivered regularly by the police to the Home from that day on. Doubtless the police were only too thankful to be relieved of their responsibilities towards the stray dogs of London. In 1870 a firm arrangement was made on behalf of the police authorities by Superintendent Kettle of Scotland Yard with the Committee of the Home:

That all dogs taken up by the Police should be sent direct to the Home, with the understanding that in all cases they would be kept for three days before being destroyed or otherwise disposed of; that no payment should be made on either side in reference to any dog consigned to the Home; that the Manager should be unrestricted as to any subsequent dealings with the dogs remaining in the Home's hands, after the expiration of three days in each case.

That order formed the basis of all future contracts that have been made with the police authorities, and which continue to this day. The Dogs' Home, Battersea, undertakes the statutory duties of the Metropolitan and City Police, whereby they take in and keep all stray dogs found in a prescribed area that stretches from Barnet in the north down to Croydon in the south, and across from Uxbridge to Dagenham, the size of a small county and covering 190 police stations. These dogs are now kept for seven clear days, and if they remain unclaimed, they become the absolute and legal property of the Dogs' Home, thus obviating the legal problems which arise when, as occasionally does happen, the original owners turn up after a dog has already been sold to a new home.

In the early days the Home also accepted a limited number of boarders, and the prices they charged, which seem laughable nowadays, ranged from two shillings a week for terriers, small spaniels, etc., three shillings for greyhounds, pointers, etc., to the colossal sum of four shillings a week for newfoundlands, mastiffs, etc.! However, when one remembers that a workman's average weekly wage was counted in shillings – four shillings a day being a usual amount – these figures do not seem so ridiculously low. The greatest worry the Committee had to face in regard to their canine paying guests was the fact that numbers of owners deposited their dogs and vanished, leaving the animals to be an indefinite drain on the limited resources of the Home. This was prudently countered by a demand for a month's board in advance before any dog could be accepted.

Although by the end of the 1860s the Home was finding itself on much firmer financial foundations, another and perhaps even greater difficulty was presenting itself.

The Home was situated in what was a densely populated district of a largely middle-class residential character, and a constant stream of complaints was being received from the local householders regarding the unbearable noise made by the legions of dogs. That these complaints were based on a reasonable foundation is undoubtedly true, for the number of dogs taken into the Home during August 1869 was 851. This number represented the average monthly intake, and that means that more than ten thousand dogs were crowding into Hollingsworth Street each year, a rate of two hundred every week. Imagine the scene of confusion that must have existed daily in that narrow little street, as the wretched and often reluctant animals arrived, some being dragged on pieces of string, some being carried in injured, others brought by coach or carriage – and probably wheelbarrow and dustcart as well.

After the poor animals had been received into the Home and had the metal numbered tag tied round their necks, they would lift their heads and cry their woes to the skies. Multiply these demented howls by fifty, and it is easy to see that the locals had reasonable grounds for complaint as they tried to go about their daily lives, deafened by the battery of noise that echoed out across their gardens and backyards.

Although at first the Committee were prepared to fight the court orders that they were receiving for nuisance, eventually they were obliged to face facts and recognize that the time had come to make a move. A sub-committee consisting of The Hon. William Byng,[1] Mr Parkinson, Mr Nugent and Mr Warriner was formed and given the unenviable task of choosing a site in London where the dawn chorus, the nightly chant and the general comings and goings at the Dogs' Home could worry no one and give rise to no complaints.

They were faced with a pretty problem, for in the rapidly growing city there were beginning to be few corners left that could measure up to the exacting requirements of an expanding Dogs' Home. It was essential that the site should be isolated enough to avoid any possible repetition of the trouble they were experiencing in Holloway, yet at the same time it had not only to be easily accessible, but also reasonably central.

After an anxious search, however, the four men reported back to the Committee in a remarkably short time that they thought they had been successful in finding exactly the right place. A triangular piece of ground of roughly half an acre was available close to Battersea Park.[2] This site was flanked by the main road on one side – a great convenience – and the lines of the London and South-Eastern Railway on the other two, thus offering the Home what was virtually an island site, with neighbours who were hardly in a position to complain of noise.

A general visit of inspection was hastily arranged, the Committee expressed themselves satisfied with the site, and

[1] Second son of the 1st Earl of Strafford, he married Flora Fox of Wellingborough, Northants, and probably met Edward Bates in consequence. His sister was married to the member of Parliament for Tufnell Park, the constituency in which the Dogs, Home lay.

[2] Battersea Park had been opened in 1858 on land that had been built up by the river largely with earth provided from the excavations for the Surrey Commercial Docks.

21

a deposit of £100 was paid on 7 May 1870 as the first instalment on the sum of £1,500 that was being asked for the land. It is interesting to know that land in that district is now fetching more than £50,000 an acre.

A firm of architects, Messrs Payne & Clarke, submitted a set of plans to the Committee which again met with general aproval, and tenders for the building of the new kennels were invited. The lowest tender was for £1,680 which was presented by a Mr Tully of Dalston, so he was duly appointed as the builder of the new Home, and instructed to put the work in hand just as soon as the Committee could make arrangements to raise the necessary funds.

It is surprising to relate that no general appeal for donations was made at this time with the specific object of raising money for the building of the new Home. The Committee had shown themselves aware of the value of advertising that same year by putting notices in *The Times, Standard, The Daily Telegraph* and *The Echo* asking owners of lost dogs to communicate with the Home, as their animals might possibly be found there, and similarly worded posters had been put up at all the main-line stations. Such general interest was being shown in the Dogs' Home and there was beginning to be such a widespead feeling of goodwill permeating towards it, that for the Committee to have missed such a fund-raising opportunity must have been a grave error of judgement. A general appeal for a building fund at that time would surely not only have resulted in a flood of donations so that sufficient money would have been raised, but many new and probably permanent supporters would have been attracted to the Home, which would thus have been spared a good deal of the acute financial anxiety that was to beset it in the future.

However, in the event, £1,500 was borrowed from the London and Westminster Bank of St James's Square[1] to buy the site on the security of the land at Hollingsworth Street. The property at Hollingsworth Street had been rented in the

[1] The National Westminster Bank still handles the financial affairs of the Dogs' Home, and one of its Managers, Mr C. J. Jay is the Hon. Treasurer of the Home.

first instance for the sum of £120 for the first year and £100 annually thereafter. However, in 1863, Mr Marriott, the landlord, had asked the Committee if they would like to buy the property outright for £1,030, and this they decided to do; they made a down payment of £550, leaving £480 to be paid off over the next seven years. This debt must just have been cleared when the negotiations for the purchase of the Battersea land were begun, and thus the Committee felt clear to go ahead with their plans for building the new kennels.

An army of workmen entered the site to dig the foundations of the Dogs' Home, Battersea, a range of buildings that nowadays would certainly be condemned as wholly unsuitable for the purpose for which they were intended, but which, a hundred years ago, were heralded as the last word in canine comfort.

4

The Borough of Battersea

Now we must take a look at Battersea, a name which has become synonymous with the Dogs' Home in the minds of many people, not only in this country, but all over the world, during the hundred years that the Home has been there.

The origin of the name of this ancient borough is lost in antiquity. The earliest records date from AD 693, and while in some of these early manuscripts the name is spelt Baetrice, in others it is Battlese, tradition relating that this name derived from the battles that were fought in the bed of the Thames when the tide was low and the river thus fordable. This was where Caesar's warriors were said to have marched across the riverbed[1] ten abreast in pursuit of the Britons.

William the Conqueror, on failing in his attempt to enter London, encamped at Battersea Reach, when most of the surrounding land was still dense forest where wolves, deer and wild boar roamed and were hunted. Twenty years later, Battersea was to appear in the Domesday Book in the Hundred of Brixton under the name of Patricesey, said to mean St Peter's Isle, the manor having been assigned for the maintenance of the Abbey of St Peter at Westminster, as it remained until the dissolution of the monasteries, when it became crown property.

In 1610 the income from the manor was applied to the maintenance of King Charles I when he was Prince of Wales, until 1627 after he had succeeded to the throne. He then

[1] Caesar (De Bell. Gall. v. II) says that at the time of his invasion the river was called Tamesis.

granted the reversion in fee of the manor of Battersea to Oliver St John, Viscount Granderson, in whose family it remained until 1763, when the whole estate was sold to Earl Spencer for £30,000.

In 1570, the greater part of lower Battersea was under water, the land that now forms the park being a boggy marsh. When the tide was high the water constantly breached the banks and flooded the surrounding land, so a great wall was built, the land drained and reclaimed.

The river, of course, has always played an important part in the lives of the inhabitants of Battersea, whose northern boundary it forms, and by 1600 when there were the names of forty thousand boatmen on the rolls of the Watermen's Company, many of them lived in Battersea, plying their trade up and down the waterway, for the River Thames was the great highway of London for hundreds of years.

Very little changed in the borough from the seventeenth century until early in the nineteenth century when London first began to extend her boundaries far beyond the city limits. Battersea was one of the many parishes dotted about on the outskirts of the big city, and there were orchards and market gardens where the Dog's Home now stands, and meadows flanking the roads. The Battersea gardeners were famous for their produce which had been commanding high prices ever since market gardening was first introduced in England in 1590[1] when they began to challenge the trade from France and Holland. It was they who first cultivated asparagus in this country and took it to the London markets.

Westminster Bridge was opened in 1750, but above that the River Thames was not spanned for many miles. Ten years later, in 1760, the tradesmen of Battersea started to feel that it was time that a bridge was built to connect their borough with Fulham. This project met with bitter opposition from across the river, where the tradesmen of Chelsea and Fulham feared that such a bridge would draw their business away. The Battersea people were determined however, and after

[1] Sherwood Ramsey, *Historic Battersea*, 1913.

many fierce arguments they finally won the day, though it took them ten years to persuade their neighbours on the north of the river that far from drawing trade away, such a bridge would bring in a constant stream of new and hitherto untapped custom.

The actual building of the bridge was watched with keen interest from both sides of the river, crowds of people congregating on the banks each day to mark its progress as the sixteen piers were raised and the wooden structure took shape. Its opening in 1771 was made an occasion of great festivity when the new bridge was hung with flags and coloured bunting and garlanded with flowers, and everybody turned out from both sides of the river to join in the merry-making.

Three years later, in 1774, river sports were introduced into England from Venice where they had been a marked feature of canal life for centuries and the subject of many well-known pictures by Canaletto and Guardi. The first regatta to take place in this country was at Battersea Reach on 23 June 1775, and once again the crowds came out in their thousands, this time to watch the spectacle of exciting races between sailing vessels and between rowing boats. This Thames regatta became an annual event, and Battersea Bridge was always crowded with spectators who paid handsomely for their vantage points. Those great summer regattas between London Bridge and Hammersmith went on until well into the nineteenth century and were to set the pattern for Henley where the first regatta was held in 1839. Each summer the river round Battersea was filled with bright craft that floated low in the water under their burdens of laughing, gaily dressed young people. They bobbed about in the wake of the paddle steamers from which the sound of brass bands rolled merrily across the water to the crowds of picnickers who lined the banks, enjoying a day's outing. Musical water parties were given on the banks of the river at Battersea during the summer, and there were pleasure gardens at the Red

House, which acted as the finishing post for many of the river sports.

However, by 1858, owing to untreated sewage being disgorged into the river, the heavier parts sinking, but the lighter ones being carried backwards and forwards on the tide, the stink from the river had become so foul that there was even talk of removing Parliament to a more healthy clime. The water supply of three million people was polluted.

Queen Victoria wrote a letter on 29 June 1858 to her daughter, the Princess Royal, who had married Prince Frederik William of Prussia earlier that year, describing a visit to Brunel's *Great Eastern,* the largest steam-vessel then designed, being 23,000 tons. Queen Victoria's letter serves to underline the condition of the river:

We went by land to Deptford yesterday, got into boats and rowed along to the Leviathan which is lying there and went on board her. . . . But we were half poisoned by the dreadful smell of the Thames—which is such that I felt quite sick when I came home, and people cannot live in their houses; the House of Commons can hardly sit—and the session will close soon in consequence. . . .

Many famous people lived in Battersea – Queen Anne spent part of her childhood in the Manor House, which was designed by Christopher Wren and built by a Huguenot refugee, Peter Paggen – but it reached the summit of its attraction as a high-class residential suburb in about 1840 when many good families had their mansions there.

Before that, as a borough, Battersea had been much disparaged, and in the early part of the nineteenth century 'Go to Battersea' was an expression used in London where nowadays people would wish to despatch their foes to a much warmer place. Undoubtedly it had its seamy side, and it was described as 'the sink-hole of Surrey'. Stewarts Lane which runs off Battersea Park Road right opposite the Dogs' Home contained so many bad characters that it became known as 'Hell's Corner', while the drinking carnivals that were held on Battersea Fields every Sunday became so rowdy that they had to be stopped. A well-known clergyman of that time, the Rev. Thomas Kirk, protested that: 'If ever there was a place out of hell, which surpassed Sodom and Gomorrah in ungodliness and abomination, this was it.' We all, of course, know what happened at Sodom, but perhaps we would have found a clue to what debaucheries were practised in Gomorrah if we had been on the river bank at Battersea in 1820.

It is at these weekly orgiastic sports that we find one of the earliest mentions of dogs in Battersea, though in 1567 the Churchwardens' accounts contain the item, 'ffor dryvyng yᵉ doges owte of yᵉ churches ijd.' and, from the beginning of the seventeenth century until after the Restoration, the 'dog-whipper' became an annual charge on the church funds. The rails around the Communion table in most Elizabethan churches were placed there, in fact, to prevent defilement of this holy place by dogs. There are entries in the Battersea Churchwarden's accounts during the plague for the killing of dogs that were considered to be 'very apt cattell to carry the infection'.

To those eighteenth-century Sunday sports then, where all kinds of contests were held, 'horse and donkey races, foot racing, walking matches, comic actors, shameless dancers, gamblers, drinking booths, and fortune-tellers' being among the many and varied amusements which drew crowds of such rough appearance and rowdy behaviour that the respectable locals kept well away, came a number of small carts drawn by dogs. These came from all over London, and some of the animals travelled more than twenty miles, being given bread soaked in some of the beer later to be consumed in great quantities by their masters, to keep up their strength on the long journeys. These carts gave rise to the expression 'dog-cart', and the dogs that drew them were strong and large, rather like a mastiff cross, being employed during the week for all kinds of light draught work. However, these big, good-natured willing animals were heartily disliked by the police in London because of the great noise they made as they went about. Their merry barks frightened the horses and added confusion to the traffic chaos that already existed and was growing daily in the city. It was for that reason as well as for humanitarian reasons, for many of the dogs were cruelly handled and exploited by their owners, that dog-carts were banned by the Metropolitan Police within a fifteen mile radius of Charing Cross. This ban became general throughout the country in 1854.

Times were to change, however, and the Red House – which had figured large in the annals of entertainment in the early nineteenth century, being the annual scene of a great sucking-pig dinner each August, and where the crack shots assembled for pigeon shooting – was closed down as Victorian reform crept into Battersea. A training college for school teachers was opened in 1842, and several schools were opened in the borough both before and after the Education Act of 1870. Until this act, which made education compulsory for all children between the ages of five and thirteen, it was estimated that only one child out of every two received any kind of education at all, and even then only the most elementary basics of the three R's.

Industries have always been important to the borough, and in 1700 potteries, cement works and breweries were in operation. Brickmaking was carried on, while whiting works and lime kilns are recorded in the parish as far back as 1650. Wickerwork baskets were made from the osiers that grew in profusion on the river banks, and there were barge builders by the river two hundred years ago, as there are now. There was a foundry at Battersea in about 1660 which cast shot for the Tower of London, and crucibles were manufactured by Morgans on the river front. Crucible-making is a very ancient art, for we know that crucibles were used in the twelfth century by the old alchemists when they tried to turn metal into gold. For scientific research the crucible has occupied an important place in history, having been aptly described as the cradle of experimental chemistry.

Paint and varnish were manufactured in Battersea where

there are paint works to this day. Sir Mark Brunel had his veneer works and saw-mills near the old Battersea Bridge, but unfortunately they were destroyed by fire in 1814. A writer described watching planks of mahogany and rosewood being sawn into veneers one-sixth of an inch thick 'with a precision, speed and grandeur of action which were really sublime'.

The Huguenots brought the art of silk-making to Battersea in 1639 at a factory which closed two hundred years later on the decline of the silk trade, and the buildings were then converted for glove-making.

Back in 1750 an industry was started in the district by the son of a French refugee, Stephen Janssan, which was destined to become famous throughout the art world, even though financially it was a failure, and the works had to be closed down ten years later. This was Battersea Enamel – enamel work on a copper base. Among all old enamels, the work done at Battersea during those few years stands out in beauty of colour, clarity of decoration and exquisite workmanship.

Quaint wooden windmills stood all along the banks of the Thames in the early part of the nineteenth century, and were a feature of the landscape at Battersea. The most famous of all was one that stood near the old parish church, and this mill was built on a new and original plan, for it was without visible sails, but had on each side a number of vertical shutters. Built in 1788, it was known as the horizontal air mill. The following description of this novel and, sad to relate, unsuccessful, mill comes from an old news sheet:

On the site of the venerable family mansion of Henry St John, Viscount Bolingbroke, is erected a horizontal air-mill, for grinding malt for distillation, originally intended for grinding linseed; it is one hundred and forty feet high, and the average diameter of the cone is about fifty feet, having ninety-six shutters, which, though only nine inches broad, reach to the height of eighty feet: these, by means of a rope, open and shut in the manner of Venetian blinds. In the inside the main shaft of the mill is the centre of a large

Sale of vagrant dogs in Chelsea in 1868, not far from the site where the Dogs' Home was to move three years later. These dogs were often stolen property and sold by the police to defray expenses

The only known picture of the dogs at Hollingsworth Street before the Home was moved to Battersea in 1871

The dog-cart was a feature of the landscape in the early nineteenth century

Queen Victoria with Tsar Nicholas II and the Tsarina (behind the Queen) and her dogs at Balmoral in 1896

Photograph from Queen Victoria's album of HRH The Princess Alice, Countess of Athlone, at the age of three or four, with Skippy, the dog believed to be the one her father, Prince Leopold, Duke of Albany, took from the Dogs' Home a few weeks after she was born in 1883

View of the kennels that were made underneath the railway arches. These are still in use

Whittington Lodge, the Cats' Home, pre-1914

One of the collecting-dogs that were a feature of the Home before the First World War

The Dogs' Home has run its own fleet of vans since 1909 when this photograph was taken

Sir Ernest Shackleton's ship, the *Endurance*, during the 1914 expedition (see chapter 13). The dogs were quartered in kennels on deck

The abandoned wreck of the *Endurance* in 1915, crushed by pack-ice

A picture from the 1920s: 'No, that isn't my dog'

Also from the 20s: Reunited!

Relations with the police have always been good. One policeman alone was responsible for bringing in 130,000 dogs from 1883 to 1903

A tempting offer that can lead to tragedy once the Christmas spirit wears off. This is the type of dog that finds itself on the streets in the New Year

circle, formed by the sails, which consist of ninety-six double planks, placed perpendicularly, and the same height as the shutters; through these shutters the wind passing turns the mill with great rapidity, which is increased or diminished by opening or shutting the apertures; in it are six pairs of stones. Adjacent are extensive bullock-houses capable of holding six hundred and fifty bullocks, to be fed with the grains from the distillery, mixed with meal.

The mill eventually closed down, and no more were built to that novel design, though many of the old prints of Battersea show that mill, and others show the windmill pump erected on Wandsworth Common by William Watson nearly thirty years later in 1815 for the purpose of supplying what was known as the 'black sea' pond with water. Mills for grinding corn at Battersea were recorded in Domesday Book, and Ranks, the well-known flour millers, have premises in the borough now.

Battersea has long been associated with the making of light, and in 1774 Joseph Bowley came from Nottingham and started a business of soap and candle-making in Westminster, moving it over to Battersea in 1868. Bowley's were later able to claim the distinction of having literally set the Thames on fire, for in 1906 nearly half their entire works were burnt down, the oils and spirit gushing into the river and spreading great sheets of flame across the water.

It was in Battersea that Price's Patent Candle Company opened a small factory in 1843 which they ran in conjunction with another works in Vauxhall. Price's were excellent employers and well in advance of their time, for not only did they open the first factory school in England where their employees were able to attend evening classes, but at their works near Liverpool the company built 140 cottages, a school, a lecture hall and a church in 1853. To this complex of buildings they added a library and a cottage hospital a few years later. At the same time, in Battersea they established a 'Workers' Pension Fund', providing the necessary capital themselves, and they inaugurated an institute that provided a library and recreation clubs, together with sewing and singing classes for the girls.

Price's also performed another, and perhaps an even more important social service, albeit quite unwittingly, for because of the enormous demand for palm oil, which grew from 19,800 tons in 1840 to nearly 50,000 tons by 1871, the tribal chiefs and kings along the west coast of Africa began to take thought. It suddenly became evident to them that their subjects were of even greater value to them when they were collecting palm oil than they were when they were sold into slavery.

How pleased William Wilberforce would have been had he lived to know this. He spent fifty years of his life in Battersea, and devoted much of his time and energy to working for the abolition of slavery. It is particularly interesting for us to know that he also played an active part in the establishment in 1824 of the Royal Society for the Prevention of Cruelty to Animals, so the Dogs' Home would have been a cause close to his heart.

In 1857, the London Gas Light Company erected works in Nine Elms Lane which were the largest in England at that time, and gave employment to some four hundred men. The tallest shaft reached 135 feet, and was so large in area that when it had been built and the final brick laid, sixteen of the workmen were given a triumphant meal of celebration on the summit.

The use of gas was strongly opposed in London at first as being of great public danger, and when it was proposed to light the House of Commons with gas, a member stood up and moved, absolutely seriously, that the pipe conveying the gas to the burners should be fixed three inches from the walls as a precaution against fire.

In 1930 work began on the gargantuan Battersea Power Station. Designed by Sir Giles Gilbert Scott of Waterloo Bridge fame, it was the first architect-designed power station in the world, and now dominates the landscape behind the Dogs' Home.

This then was Battersea, where the Home for Lost and Starving Dogs was to open its doors on 3 June 1871, doors which have remained open ever since.

5

The First Decade at Battersea

In 1871, Battersea was a small parish of some twelve thousand inhabitants, and this being before the time of Borough Councils, which did not come into existence until 1899, it was under the rule of the Vestry.

The Vestry was not an elected body but was composed of every ratepayer in the parish. With the vicar as its chairman, the meetings were held in the vestry room of the parish church. The debates were often of a violently stormy character, as feelings were apt to run high, and language was used that was sadly out of keeping with the sanctified surroundings. A Highway Board and Inspectors of Lighting were elected annually by the Vestry, as were a Board of Overseers responsible for making and collecting the poor rate and tabulating the Parliamentary List. A vote at the Vestry was taken by show of hands, and then, if a poll was subsequently demanded, the churchwardens had to go in person round the parish knocking on all the doors, asking each ratepayer in turn how he wished to cast his vote on the question at issue.

This clearly was not a very satisfactory state of affairs, and it is small wonder that with a set-up of that kind, the opening of a Dogs' Home in the borough went unheralded and almost unnoticed locally.

The first committee meeting at the new premises, then, was convened on 3 June 1871. Advertisements were inserted in various newspapers to inform the public of the move, and posters and handbills were distributed all over the wide area covered by the activities of the Home, describing the new kennels as being in the Lower Wandsworth Road, Battersea and close to York Road Railway Station.

The move itself took place with the minimum of fuss, the dogs in their care at the time being transported by hired vans, and Keeper Pavitt and his family moved into quarters near to the new Home. The Holloway premises were left empty.

The motto of the Home might well have repeated the slogan of the Windmill Theatre of war-time fame, 'We never closed', for although visiting times have always had to be fixed for the general public coming to the Home with the idea of buying a new pet, no owner genuinely seeking a lost dog has ever been refused admission when he has arrived at a reasonable time during the day except possibly in times of national emergency, and of course the work with the dogs is carried on all day and every day.

As with all new buildings, faults were not slow to show themselves, and by the end of the first year it was obvious that, with the rapidly growing amount of traffic around the Home, it would be advisable to have the grounds concreted over. This work was put in hand, and when completed made a great difference to the daily work of the kennelmen.

The Home had opened with one huge exercise yard, on the lines of the one so vividly described in the article published in Charles Dickens' journal. This was designed to serve all the inmates of the kennels, but it was found that this great wide open space – this lovely playground which seemed to offer a delightful amount of freedom to the animals, a freedom that had been out of the question at Holloway – in practice produced problems of its own. Once out in that vast yard, the dogs went mad, rushing round, leaping about, fighting and barking, and when the time came for that particular batch to be shut up again, to give the new lot their turn for exercise, it took the hot and sweating kennelmen a very long time to round up their charges and see that they went into the right kennel. No doubt by the time the doors were slammed behind the last gaily wagging tail, not only were the kennelmen far better exercised than the dogs, but they had probably taught their charges language that would have made the ladies on the Committee gasp and stretch their eyes, and perhaps even have given the Battersea Vestry cause for surprise. Judging from early photographs of the staff at the Home, particularly Keeper Pavitt who must have weighed at least 250 pounds, they were not built for violent exercise.

The Committee decided to split up the yard so that each section of the kennels had its own adjoining exercise yard into which the dogs could go at will. Corrugated iron shelters were also erected under which the dogs could shelter from the sun and the rain, and thus life was made easier and more comfortable for them.

At the same time it was decided to build a new kennel to house the smaller dogs, for however perky and bold a small dog may have been and generally was, he was literally outweighed in size, and must have found himself overwhelmed by his large and often exuberant companions. Space was already at a premium, but somebody had the bright idea that the adjacent railway arches might be put to good use, and so the first of these arches was rented and used for storage.

A short while later the ground in front of the straw store was becoming very worn in spite of the concreting, so it was paved and a tramway was laid in the passage leading to the gates. This enabled the bulky loads of food and bedding that arrived daily to be moved about more easily.

As early as 1874 the whole premises were repainted, and it was then that a pattern was set that has been followed throughout the years whereby all the maintenance jobs wherever possible are carried out by the staff, outside help only being called in when skilled labour is absolutely essential.

In 1878 more improvements were carried out; all the footpaths around the Home were paved and drained, and the boundary wall on the north side, the railway and river side, was raised to provide more shelter for the dogs in their exercise yards. At the same time it was decided to put new windows in all the buildings, thus giving more light which would enable owners to identify their pets more easily, and would also improve the ventilation. Five hundred dogs kept in confined conditions with very little air circulating must have produced a somewhat rarified atmosphere. Another range of sheds was added to the existing buildings, thus enabling 550 dogs to be housed at any one time.

In the following year, 1879, a kennel with twenty-four separate compartments was built on the only remaining spare piece of ground. This was designed specifically for animals that were in need of special care and attention, such as bitches in whelp and dogs that had been brought in as a result of accidents.

Numbers were soaring, for in 1880 nearly nineteen thousand dogs passed through the Home during the year. It is extraordinary to relate that this is the level at which the average yearly intake has remained from that day.

The Home was becoming famed and respected, not only in England, but also abroad, visitors coming to see it from all over he world. In an article written for the *Cologne Gazette* some years later, Dr Carl Schneider gave a moving description of his visit to Battersea.

It is an ear-splitting concert, performed as soon as any new arrival is perceived, with the pertinacity of despair, for it is sheer despair that is depicted on most of the canine faces, despair at the discomforts of confinement, the unaccustomed surroundings, the impending doom. I shall not forget for a long time to come, the look on the face of an aristocratic collie; he looked at me with human eyes, whimpering and whining and unfolding his troubles to me in exquisite dog language, moving body and tail in every possible posture of entreaty and abject submission, and, when I moved away, he pressed his nose and paws against the railings and emitted a cry such as might burst from the ship-wrecked mariner on a barren island, who sees the sail on which he built his hopes of deliverance disappear on the horizon. . . . When a dog is claimed, the meeting between master and dog is a most touching scene. As soon as the animal hears the sound of his master's voice, he jumps about as if demented, then circles around him with mad leaps, his eyes sparkle with joy, and, when he has been redeemed, he rushes out without even casting a farewell look upon his less fortunate fellow prisoners.

However, financial problems loomed large during that first decade, and in November 1871, only a matter of months after the new kennels had been opened, the Committee members found themselves obliged to go to the money market. The premises at Holloway remained unsold, and although there was an occasional enquiry from a would-be purchaser, they were unable to find anybody who was willing to make them a firm offer, and their creditors were beginning to be pressing.

It must have been extremely distasteful for the Committee to be reduced to such straits, but it looked to them as if there was no alternative. They therefore borrowed £4,000 at the then exorbitant rate of interest of ten per cent per annum partly on the security of the deeds of the Holloway property and partly on the security of the deeds of the Battersea property, from the British Mutual Society. They were evidently involving themselves in some very tricky financial negotiations, for it will be remembered that £1,500 had already been borrowed from the London and Westminster Bank on the security of the land at Hollingsworth Street, backed by a collateral promissory note signed by five male members of the Committee. Here they were, less than a year later, borrowing a further sum from a different source on the same security. No doubt the bank loan was repaid at the same time.

The sale of the Holloway property still hung fire, nobody appearing to be anxious to buy it until 1874 when it was eventually sold for the knock-down price of £900 which represented a loss of more than £200 on the land alone, without taking into account the improvements that had been made. When we learn that the buyer was none other than Mr James Johnson, the recently promoted Manager and Secretary of the

Home, who had come to Holloway as Superintendent in 1865, we begin to wonder what in fact was going on. Had Johnson deliberately withheld offers from the ears of the Committee in order to pull the price of the property down until it came within his financial reach? Of course, we shall never know the answer to this question, and the man therefore must be given the benefit of the doubt, especially in view of the fact that he died three years later in 1877.

He seems to have had the Committee in the palm of his hand, however, for they were obliged to borrow a further £100 from him to enable them to pay off £2,000 to the investment company, who would not release the Holloway deeds for less. A windfall in the form of a legacy of £1,000 from Mrs Hambleton who had opened the original subscription list with two guineas made up the amount required, and the sale was thus able to be completed.

It must have been a desperately worrying time for them all, and from a distance of a hundred years it looks as if they were all pitifully naive and, while proving themselves capable of founding and running the Home, were otherwise completely unversed in business matters. However, in 1876 one of the lady members of the Committee, Miss Lloyd, came forward with a solution, making a suggestion that was seized upon gratefully by the rest of the Committee. Miss Lloyd offered to take over the mortgage on the property at Battersea from the investment company, thus releasing the deeds of the premises from their hands. What is more, she declared that she would be happy to take only five per cent interest, which halved the interest payments. A legacy was expected shortly from a Dr Gibson, and the Committee, who must have been severely shaken by then, wisely decided to use this money to reduce their debt to Miss Lloyd. Although the legacy did not materialize until the following year, when it did come it amounted to £800, thus reducing the outstanding debt to £1,200, a much more manageable sum.

The day to day running of the Home must have swallowed up all the donations and subscriptions that came in, for whatever the basic financial problems were, the fact remained that wages had to be paid each week and the monthly bills met. It was decided to make another appeal in 1878 to follow the one made three years earlier that had brought in nearly a hundred pounds.

These money problems caused a heavy cloud to lie blanketing the Home for many years, and a rumour that was spread by the newspapers in 1886, totally without foundation, to the effect that a legacy of £10,000 had been received, led to subscriptions falling to almost nothing, and two further loans of £500 each had to be obtained from the bank.

However, by 1880 things started to look up and money began to come in an ever increasing stream. At last the Dogs' Home, Battersea, was becoming solvent.

6

More Problems: Vivisection

No history of the Dogs' Home would be complete without a mention of that vexing question, vivisection, and it was in 1875 that the first rumours of a whispering campaign were heard at Battersea. These whispers were to persist constantly throughout the next twenty-five years, and intermittently after that, right down to the present day. It was being said that the dogs at the Home were sold to laboratories for the purposes of experiment.

Nothing could be further from the truth, for it must be remembered that one of the firmest principles on which the Home was founded, and one that has been strictly adhered to ever since, was that no animal would, knowingly to the Committee, end up on the vivisectionist's table or be used for experiment.

The annual report of the Home carries the following paragraph each year:

Each purchaser is required to sign a form absolving the Committee from all responsibility with regard to the dog, stating the purpose for which the animal is required, *undertaking that it shall not be used for the purposes of vivisection* nor as a performing dog, and further stating that he is not a dealer nor the agent of a dealer.

The entire object of the institution was and always has been to save dogs from a lingering death in the streets of London; so to bring the dogs into the Home, restore them to health, and then sell them for experimentation would have defeated the object entirely.

As early as 1868, before the move to Battersea, a written application was received from a Mr Murphy, resident surgeon at the Royal Free Hospital. He asked if he could be supplied with dogs from the Home to be used in experiments at his hospital. The Committee were appalled, and with horror and indignation they immediately referred the matter to Mr John Colam, secretary of the RSPCA, who immediately sent off an inspector to explain the situation to Mr Murphy.

John Colam must have been a man of outstanding character; secretary of the RSPCA and editor of *Animal World*, the official organ of that society, as a young man he had been one of the prime movers in abolishing the vicious sport of cock-fighting, and in 1870 he was instrumental in nipping in the bud an attempt to establish bull-fighting in this country by leaping into the arena at the Agricultural Hall, Islington, where a demonstration by Spanish matadors was taking place, thus breaking up the performance. He narrowly escaped lynching by the angry spectators, but he won the day, for the matadors were fined and expelled from the country, and the prospect of bull-fighting becoming a national sport in England from that day ceased to exist.

Relationships between the RSPCA and the Dogs' Home had always been cordial and in the early days the Committee meetings of the Home were conducted at 105 Jermyn Street, the premises of the RSPCA. In 1888, when the Home had found itself in severe financial straits, the RSPCA had come to the rescue, thanks to the good offices of Sir George Measom who was chairman of both bodies, with an interest-free loan of £1,000, which the Home was able to repay the following year.

After the Royal Free Hospital case, the Committee determined never to allow a dog to go to anyone giving a hospital as their address, and a few years later, as an additional safeguard, would-be visitors who wished to see the dogs had to apply for a pass in the office before being allowed through to the yard. This led to the staggering discovery that up to forty thousand people were visiting the Home annually.

In 1875 the Committee employed a Scotland Yard detective
to clear them conclusively of the many accusations being
levelled against them that they were providing dogs for
vivisection, and eight years later, in 1883, another detective
was employed to follow up the animals that were sold by the
Home. The result of this further investigation was completely
reassuring.

Vivisection, of course, in the 1870s was a very different
thing from the experiments carried on in this country today.
Thanks to the efforts of bodies such as the RSPCA and the
independent anti-vivisection societies over the years, no
reputable laboratory would now entertain the idea of taking
animals for experimental purposes other than from known
sources. Indeed, many laboratories breed a variety of
animals for themselves, or obtain them from approved
breeders of repute.

The very word 'vivisection' is misleading when it is applied
to what happens in laboratories now, for the word literally
means the cutting, *sectio,* of living, *vivus,* animals. This then
is a word that is equally applicable to all surgical operations,
whether upon man or beast and for whatever purpose. In
point of fact, the conventional use of the word refers only to
animals other than man in relation to the advancement of
medical and scientific knowledge.

The question of vivisection produces difficult moral problems. However, the average person is a realist, and it is
obvious that if medicine and science are to progress, then
certain experiments requiring living tissue must be carried
out. On the whole it is desirable that this living tissue should
belong to what are commonly called animals of the lower
orders. It is by no means unheard of, though, for scientists and
doctors to experiment upon themselves and upon selected
volunteers, but generally speaking a variety of animals are
used such as dogs, cats, monkeys, rats, mice, rabbits and
guinea-pigs. Sheep, pigs, cows, donkeys and horses are also
used occasionally, particularly when the effects of certain
chemicals on grazing animals are required to be known.

Controlled experiments on animals have been found to be fully justified in the light of the results they have yielded in the sciences of physiology and pathology, though there will always be some difference of opinion as to the necessity of many of the experiments.

Dr R. W. Smithells wrote in *The Practitioner* in 1965, 'It may be extremely difficult to reproduce in laboratory animals the toxic effects that a drug shows in man', and Dr P. R. Peacock was reported in the *Daily Sketch* in 1960 as saying, 'We cannot consider the laboratory animals on which we do our tests as human, and give certificates of harmlessness for men to substances tested on animals. We can never be entirely sure that the results would be the same in men.'

Not all doctors and scientists engaged in research will entirely agree with these opinions, but what all responsible doctors and scientists are agreed on is that every experiment should take place under strictly controlled conditions. With few exceptions, they are perfectly prepared to demonstrate the reason for the experiments they are undertaking, and the giving of these reasons is the strongest safeguard there could possibly be against the abuse of the practice. The reports are reassuring in that they show that often the very statistics giving the total numbers of experiments can be misleading. By far the greater number of the experiments consist in the main of genetical research, injections and diet, rather than the actual cutting into living flesh, grafting and the transmitting of deathly diseases, though many of the psychological experiments carried out today are distasteful, and seem unnecessarily callous to the layman.

It was the development of anaesthesia that was largely responsible for the growth in the number and scope of experiments on animals, because up to then it would have been impossible for many to have been carried out. By means of anaesthesia, an animal could be kept unconscious and quiet during prolonged operations. The horrifying mental picture of tormented animals literally being held down by force while the vivisectionists attacked them with scalpels can hardly

ever have been true, simply because of the practical difficulties that would have been met. Undoubtedly in days gone by
there were a great many cruel practices, and even today there
are many things that sicken the animal-lover. It must be
remembered, however, that what may seem cruel and callous
to the layman has a quite different connotation to the surgeon
and scientist, to whom by virtue of their professions the living
organism must take on a different aspect, or they would be
unable to carry out their work of healing and research.

The RSPCA sets out its policy on vivisection quite clearly as
follows:

> The RSPCA is not an abolitionist organisation. Although with an
> understandable reluctance, it accepts that some amount of animal
> experimentation is essential in the interests of human beings
> and of animals themselves—notably in curbing and ending disease.
> But the Society is firmly opposed to *all* experiments which cause
> pain and it believes that no effort and no expense should be spared
> in discovering, perfecting and applying alternative techniques
> and procedures not requiring the use of living animals. It believes,
> also, that every possible safeguard should be imposed against the
> infliction of distress and suffering, and against the needless repeti-
> tion of experiments.

This statement by the RSPCA is implemented by the stringent requirements of the Home Office. Before any hospital or
laboratory is permitted to undertake experiments on living
animals, the premises must be registered, and before registration the proposed housing is inspected. All inspections are
carried out by doctors and veterinary surgeons employed by
the Home Office who are thus qualified to understand in part
at any rate the scope of the work which is to be carried out.
They make their initial inspection with special attention to
the use of the premises for particular animals, with the wellbeing of those animals heading the list of requirements. After
registration, inspectors from the Home Office have a legal
right to enter the premises again at any time without giving
any notice. Should there be anything that the inspectors do
not like, they can and do demand that it is put right. If it is

not, then registration can be withdrawn and work in that laboratory would have to cease immediately.

It is reassuring to the lay general public to know that these rights are frequently exercised, and it is equally reassuring to know that such stringent rules exist. That they do must in part of course be due to the effective 'police' forces that exist in the form of the various animal rescue and anti-vivisection societies.

The RSPCA statement does to the author's mind exactly voice the feeling of the average thinking member of society. It is obvious that a certain amount of experimentation on animals must perforce be undertaken for the benefit of mankind in general, but most people are united in a wish that the sufferings of animals should be reduced to the minimum, if it cannot be removed altogether.

It must be repeated emphatically at this point, though, that no animals from Battersea knowingly to the Committee are ever used for living laboratory experiments.

7

Royal Interest

In 1879, the Dogs' Home at Battersea received its first intima-
tion of royal interest when the Prince of Wales, later to
become King Edward VII, sent word that he proposed to visit
the home with Queen Marie of the Belgians. Queen Marie,
the wife of King Leopold II who was responsible for the
founding of the Congo Free State, was much loved in Belgium
for her beauty, her sweet character and her charm. Daughter
of the Archduke Joseph of Austria, and great-granddaughter
of the Empress Maria Theresa, she was mother-in-law to the
Crown Prince Rudolph of tragic Mayerling fame.

When the news reached the Dogs' Home of the coming of
these royal visitors there was great excitement, and a spate
of whitewashing and scrubbing was feverishly begun. Doubtless this royal visit, like so many others, provided both the
spur and the opportunity for several pressing jobs of maintenance to be carried out in double quick time, which might
otherwise have been left for a few more months. That everything was in apple-pie order by the time the Prince of Wales
arrived is evidenced by the remarks of the Prince and Queen
Marie as they left the premises. After having made a minute
and detailed inspection, they congratulated the manager, Mr
Scoborio, the ex-RSPCA superintendent who had succeeded
Johnson, warmly on the working and general management
of the Home.

Four years later, in 1883, there came a visitor who may
have been responsible for the final seal of royal approval being
placed on the Home. This visitor was Queen Victoria's young-

est son, Prince Leopold, Duke of Albany, who, on his death, the Queen was to describe as 'the dearest of my dear sons', though when he was a child she had talked of him as 'not an engaging child, though amusing', and was to complain as he grew older that he was becoming quizzical.

Prince Leopold's story is a tragic one. Born a haemophiliac, and so delicate that he had to live a circumscribed life and be protected from bruises and falls, as a child he also suffered from a defect of tongue and speech. He must have overcome or outgrown this affliction however, for he became a polished and accomplished speaker. A man of cultivated tastes and great charm, he was described as forging a much-needed 'link between Court and culture'.

When Prince Leopold visited the Dogs' Home in 1883, he was just thirty, and had been married to Princess Helen, daughter of the reigning Prince of Waldeck and Pyrmont for about a year. The young couple had recently had their first child, Princess Alice, who when she grew up, married Prince Alexander of Teck, later created Earl of Athlone, Queen Mary's brother.

Prince Leopold, like his eldest brother, went all round the kennels looking at everything, but when he left he did not leave alone. He took away with him in his carriage a small fox-terrier. It is nice to think that he chose this dog as a pet for his new little daughter, and that it was in fact Skippy, the fox-terrier that Princess Alice says she remembers in her nursery when she was a child.

The Prince was to die within a year, but before his untimely death he must have given his mother, the Queen, a glowing report of the Dogs' Home, for Queen Victoria asked Sir Henry Ponsonby, her private secretary, to visit the Home and to report back to her on what he found there. The Queen was well known by her subjects as well as by her own family for her deep and abiding interest in the welfare of all animals, and more particularly that of dogs, to which she almost invariably referred as 'man's best friend'.

Sir Henry must have gone into every nook and cranny at

Battersea, for he had been a soldier, and his eye for detail is immediately apparent in the papers he prepared daily for the Queen. However, Queen Victoria was evidently not completely satisfied with the report he placed before her, and Sir Henry was obliged to return.

This time all was well, for on 22 December 1885 the Queen wrote one of her frequent memoranda to her private secretary, asking him to send a donation to the Home, and to indicate to them that she would like to give a further similar sum annually.[1]

Sir Henry replied promptly to her the next day saying that he had sent a sum of money to the Home, and had in accordance with her orders informed the secretary that Her Majesty would like to give a similar sum each year.[2]

That Sir Henry was a master of diplomacy in his capacity as adviser to the Queen is evident, for he added with both wisdom and caution, that as Her Majesty had mentioned two figures, he had taken the lower one, as the donation could always be increased in the future.

At the bottom of this note from Sir Henry, the Queen wrote how distressed she was at the fact that the dogs were destroyed after three days, and she wished they could be kept for up to ten days, when she would gladly give more.

The Committee at Battersea were, of course, overjoyed by this evidence of royal approval, as the following extract from the Chairman's speech at the Twenty-fifth Annual General Meeting shows:

Last year we expressed our satisfaction at the important fact that His Royal Highness the Prince of Wales had become one of our subscribers. This year we are in a position to state that Her Most Gracious Majesty the Queen has not only sent a donation, but has kindly added her name to the list of subscribers. . . . Twice during the past year the Institution was visited by Sir Henry Ponsonby, and on both occasions at the request of the Queen. It is a source of great congratulation to know that not only has Her

[1] RA P.P. 1/6 2
[2] RA P.P. 1/6 3

Majesty become a pecuniary supporter of the Home showing sympathy with our work, but she has also given evidence of her approval of our Management of the Institution, both donation and subscription having been paid after the visits of Sir Henry Ponsonby. As the arm of justice, we are told, is long enough to reach the wrongdoer, so the tender heart of our beloved Queen goes out toward suffering whether felt by man or beast. It is almost impossible to speak without a feeling of emotion concerning the Queen of these Realms. Every day some fresh instance occurs of her goodness, not only to her people, but, when within her power, to all created things in the United Kingdom.

Five years later, this chairman, George Measom, JP, was to receive the honour of a knighthood for his services, not only as Chairman of the Dogs' Home, but more particularly as Chairman of the RSPCA, of which body Queen Victoria had been Patron since 1835, two years before she succeeded to the throne. It is sad that we have no record of Sir George's transportations of delight on the receipt of his accolade at the hand of his beloved Monarch.

After the Annual General Meeting, a careful letter was drafted by the Committee to Sir Henry Ponsonby in which they asked if the Queen would be gracious enough to grant her patronage to the Home. It was pointed out that patronage had been granted by both her sons who had visited them. This request was passed on immediately to Queen Victoria by Sir Henry, and she wrote across the top of his note the words: 'Most certainly. *No one loves* Dogs more than The Queen or would wish to do more to promote their comfort and happiness. They are man's *truest* friends.'[1]

Queen Victoria's views about the length of time that dogs should be kept had been passed on to the Committee, and this time was immediately increased from three days to five. Lord Onslow,[2] who was president of the Home for five years before he became Governor-General of New Zealand, pointed out in a letter from Clandon Park to Sir Henry Ponsonby[3] that

[1] RA P.P. 1/6 4
[2] Lord Onslow had been a lord in waiting on the Queen.
[3] RA P.P. 1/6 7

50

the Home must of necessity be in a position to destroy some of the animals after three days. In a few instances dogs came into the place in such a pitiful state that to destroy them as soon as possible was the most merciful action. He also pointed out that the new five-day limit would, in practice, mean that most of the dogs had a stay of sentence of nearly a week, as the first day was not counted, and those that remained unclaimed were not destroyed until the morning of the seventh.

The warm-hearted Queen had evidently given a great deal of thought to the fate of 'her beloved dogs'[1] 'who surely have souls'.[2] Her wish was naturally felt to be the Committee's command, but this extension of time for the dogs led to what virtually amounted to a state of emergency at Battersea. The Home was crowded out as it was, owing to a police order for the seizure of dogs found in the streets not under control, and almost overnight the daily numbers swelled from 500 to 750, and there simply was not enough room to house the influx. However, more railway arches were hastily rented from the London, Dover and Chatham Railway and converted into emergency kennels.

Queen Victoria was to continue both her patronage and her interest in the Home until her death in 1901. King Edward VII on his succession to the throne, graciously consented to become Patron once more, an office he had dropped when his mother, the Queen, had taken it on.

In the jubilee year of the Home, King Edward VII died, but the royal patronage was to be continued by his son, King George V, and on 18 May 1956, our present monarch, Queen Elizabeth II, became the second reigning queen to grant her patronage to the Dogs' Home, Battersea.

[1] RA Add. A/12 1314
[2] RA P.P. 1/6 2

8

The Great Rabies Scare

It will be remembered that the dogs found on the street and brought to the Home were in fact the statutory responsibility of the police; but no payment was made by them for the service rendered by the Dogs' Home until the year 1878, when they sent a donation of ten guineas to the funds of the Home in respect of the additional work that had been undertaken on their behalf during the preceding year.

In 1876 the police had offered to pay threepence per dog, but what they gave with their strong right arm they took away with their left, for at the same time they required the secretary of the Home to make a reciprocal payment to the police of exactly the same sum of threepence for each dog they brought in. This meant that the Home lost a possible £225 a year, having regard to the fact that about eighteen thousand dogs were being handled annually.

In 1877 the police had been obliged to put out a general order to the effect that owing to the number of complaints they were receiving about dangerous dogs at large in the suburban districts, all dogs would be seized that were found not to be under proper control within the Metropolitan Police district. Before making this order, the cooperation of the Dogs' Home was assured by getting their agreement to deal with the large numbers of dogs that would be bound to arrive as a result.

This police order was the first of several, and heralded a rabies scare that was to sweep the country, bringing untold suffering to countless animals; for the scare brought a panic in its wake that led to scenes of appalling brutality. The police were under orders to destroy any dog suspected of harbouring the dread disease, and as they could not carry poison and were forbidden either to carry firearms or to use knives, they were obliged to bludgeon the poor animals to death. This led to horrifying scenes as they carried out their task, egged on by the sort of vicious crowd that will always gather to witness any act of brutality.

In 1881 the Committee of the Dogs' Home sent a letter to the newspapers for publication, from which the following extract serves to underline what was happening all over London, when a good many 'confirmed' cases of rabies were nothing of the sort and probably merely cases of hysteria or epilepsy:

Ignorance of the real symptoms of rabies will inevitably lead to atrocities in our streets. A fit is not a symptom, as is popularly supposed, and no alarm ought to be felt by the public when they see a convulsed dog in the street. Unfortunately, people do not stop to reason, but give way to their fears, when they see such an occurrence, and the poor brute is consequently driven up one street and down another at the utmost speed, kicked, stoned, terrorised and maddened into fury, until he bites someone obstructing or pursuing him, whereupon without further evidence he is pronounced mad. . . . A few days ago, as a policeman was bringing in a half-breed homeless pug to Battersea, the animal had a fit in a street adjacent to the Home. The cry was set up—'Kill him, he is mad.' 'Knock his brains out.' 'If he bites you, you are a dead man,' etc. Fortunately the dog was taken up by one of our keepers, whose experience enabled him to make a correct diagnosis of the dog's complaint. The dog was brought to the Home where medicine was administered and kindness bestowed upon him. It soon recovered and was subsequently sent to a good home and a kind mistress.

This pug was more fortunate than a little spaniel that became the subject of a court case and scandal of such dimensions that it came to the ears of the Queen herself. This was known as 'The Baker Street "Mad-dog" Case' and happened in July 1886. A small dog, said to be in perfect health, was turned out for an airing, complete with muzzle, from the front door of a house in Baker Street, where its owner was staying for a few days. The muzzle had been chafing, and the dog started to rub its mouth on the railings. A lady who saw this from her window opposite, ran down, adjusted the muzzle and patted the dog. However, her act of kindness was evidently seen by a man who promptly went round to the local police station to report that there was a rabid dog at large in Baker Street.

Within a matter of minutes the police had arrived with their lassoes, and between them they beat the poor unfortunate little animal to death with their truncheons on the steps of a house. Hearing the dog's pitiful cries, the woman who owned the house came rushing out, but unable to persuade the police to stop, she ran upstairs and in desperation poured water on the head of the chief offender, and it was this act that made her liable to an action for assault.

The ladies concerned wrote to the Queen, giving her a graphic description of the whole affair, and describing the dog as 'a gentle, quiet and affectionate little animal'.[1] The Queen was so upset that she demanded a full and immediate enquiry at the highest level.[2]

The Home Secretary, Godfrey Lushington, pointed out that the case had been tried in open court, where each party had had full opportunity to give evidence. A charge of cruelty against the police was dismissed, and the lady concerned was fined for assault, and this seemed to him to be conclusive.[3] Sir Charles Warren, Chief Commissioner of the Metropolitan Police, produced a plausible list of remarks and observations which must have served to allay the worry of the Queen;[4] yet somehow an examination of the facts today leaves one with the unpleasant feeling that a hasty curtain was drawn over the truth to spare the feelings of the Queen, for there

[1] RA P.P. 1/6 24
[2] RA P.P. 1/6 34
[3] RA P.P. 1/6 37
[4] RA P.P. 1/6 36

seems to be a false ring about the evidence produced for her, and she was right to worry about the brutalizing effects that the order was having on the police.

A further rabies order in 1889-90 led to conditions of acute crisis in the Home, for the hard-driven kennelmen were called upon to handle some nine thousand additional dogs during that year. It says much for their calmness and control that they were able to cope with such an emergency with the minimum of fuss. Hundreds upon hundreds of dogs were brought in by day and night. There was nowhere to put them and nothing to feed them on. All the animals were suspected of being rabid, they were frightened and bewildered, and a good many of them must have been dangerously belligerent.

An interesting fact is that in spite of the thousands of dogs of all descriptions handled both by the police and by the staff of the Dogs' Home during those years of crisis, not one case of hydrophobia occurred, although several keepers had to undergo the prophylactic treatment then available.

Sir Charles Warren came in for a good deal of abuse from right-minded individuals who were horrified at the conditions prevailing. An open letter to him written on satirical lines was published in September 1886, and a copy was kept among Queen Victoria's papers:[1]

Sir,
All men who duly appreciate the dignity of human nature, and the sacredness of human-life, will applaud to the echo your noble, merciful, and sagacious opinion which appears in 'The Times' Newspaper of yesterday's date. Your sentiment as reported there, being—*'I am of opinion that the life of one human being is of more importance than all the Dogs in Christendom.'* The sentence is most admirable—it ought to be written in letters of gold!

But, why halt where you do? Why not say—'The life of one human being (no matter whose) is of more importance than all the Dogs, Horses, Camels, etc., etc., in Christendom?' Why not say, 'than all the animals?'

[1] RA P.P. 1/6 45

And, why confine yourself to 'Christendom', and leave out the rest of the world and all other religious beliefs?

Don't, I beg, 'make *two* bites at a cherry'. 'Go the whole animal.' 'Out-Herod Herod.' Those weak-minded men and silly women who like Dogs will of course cry out against you—but never mind them. They will bring against your noble sentiment, the opinion of Byron.

> 'The poor dog, in life the firmest friend
> The first to welcome, foremost to defend.'

And they will quote Sir Walter Scott's assertion, that 'The dog is the friend of man, except where man justly incurs his enmity.' Also, Robert Burns will be quoted, where he says 'The dog puts the Christian to shame.' But, my dear Sir Charles, regard them not, for what did Byron, Scott and Burns know about the Canine Race and Human Race, and what their comparative values are? Nothing, absolutely nothing, compared to your knowledge. There is, there can be, there shall be no doubt that the life of the basest wretch, the most atrocious miscreant that your Department—that the London Police—ever brought to Justice, is worth the lives of Landseer's Distinguished Member of the Humane Society, The Dogs of St Bernard, The Shepherd's Chief Mourner, Grey-Friars Bobby, and all the dogs who bravely saved human life at the risk of their own, or faithfully solaced the sufferings of the poor and lonely.

Your Department well remembers the late Mr Peace[1] (fortunately for honest folk now '*at* Peace'). Well, these dog-loving, dog-owning fools and fanatics will boldly assert that one honest watch-dog is of more importance than a universe of Peaces. But *we* know better, Sir Charles. Rascal, thief, burglar, and murderer out-value all the dogs in Christendom.

> 'Let Gallows gape for Dog, let Man go free.'

Go ahead, say I. Down with the Dogs. I admire the style in which you butcher them in the streets of pious London. Do all your men like the work though? Some may think that the guardians of the law ought not to be forced to do knackers' work—they may consider it brutal and degrading to manly minds. Some of the Constabulary, no doubt, are fond of animals. However, most for-

---

[1] Charlie Peace was a notorious murderer, and strange to relate in this context, his dog, which used to sit waiting for him at the scenes of his crimes, ended up at the Dogs' Home and became a trusted and much-loved watch dog.

tunately, their Head is above such weak-mindedness, and would massacre all the dogs in Christendom rather than a Mr Peace or the Netherby Hall murderers should receive one bite. I understand that the Horse Guards did not confer sufficient honours and distinctions upon you for your able conduct in South Africa—because there was no bloody engagement, no 'Butcher's Bill'. There can be no fault found with you on the present campaign, for your 'Butcher's Bill' is enormous. No Albuera or Waterloo business either, for *you* have not lost a single man—real scientific warfare yours! Have you killed any Blind-men's dogs yet? And when will you attack Foxhounds, Deerhounds, Pointers, Setters, Spaniels, Shepherd's dogs, and, lastly your Most Gracious Sovereign's Dogs? Down with them all, on principle—your principle. . . .

'Yours, with much respect and admiration,

Down-With-The-Dogs

14th September, 1886.

However unpopular and however open to abuse, the rabies orders did have a considerable measure of success in terms of a dramatic drop in the number of cases of rabies, which fell to thirty-eight in 1892, though the numbers increased to 727 in 1895 when control was returned by the police to the local authorities. There had been, of course, no statistics of the incidence of rabies in Great Britain until after the introduction of the first rabies order in 1886 which was imposed at the height of the scare, and which made muzzling compulsory for every dog in the streets. After that time, 1,583 cases were confirmed in dogs and other animals in this country before the disease was eventually eradicated in 1902, when quarantine for imported dogs was introduced.

9
Rabies

To understand the state of panic that swept the country at
the end of the last century, it is necessary to know a little
more about the disease of rabies, as it is difficult for the average person living in this country nowadays to realize what an
appalling scourge it is.

Rabies, which is the Latin for madness, is the name used for
the disease when it manifests itself in animals of various kinds
– dogs, cats, wolves, rabbits, foxes, and even horses and cows
being among the victims – whereas the word hydrophobia,
which means literally 'fear of water', from the Greek root of
the word, is the name used for the disease in humans.

It is one of the most dread diseases known to man, and
it has probably existed from time immemorial, for there is
mention of it in writings throughout the ages, in the works of
Aristotle, Xenophon, Plutarch, Virgil, Horace, Ovid and many
others, as well as in the works of early writers on medicine.
The malady has always been, and rightly so, regarded with
the utmost dread and horror, for the suffering of an infected
man or beast defies description.

In humans the early symptoms are great mental depression,
together with a restlessness that causes the patient to roam
hither and thither, unable to be still for more than a moment
or two, but at the same time uttering a constant babble of
chatter. There is feverishness, loss of appetite, sleeplessness,
headache, great nervous excitability and wheezy breathing,
together with a noticeable aversion to liquids. These symptoms continue for a couple of days, and are then followed

by a state of excitement which develops into a frenzy, the face showing anxiety and terror. By then, the most striking feature of the disease is a complete inability to swallow fluids, although there is an overwhelming thirst. Any attempt to drink only produces a violent suffocative paroxysm produced by a spasm of the muscles of swallowing and breathing, and this continues for several seconds. After a short rest, another attempt is made, but all that happens is a repetition of the first, and so it goes on until the end, when even the sound of running water may produce a paroxysm. In many cases at this stage there is maniacal excitement and belligerence, followed by calm intervals when the patient is fully aware of what is happening to him.

After two or three days of suffering of this horrifying description the patient finally dies, either in a paroxysm of choking on his own saliva, or from sheer exhaustion. Death at the end comes as a welcome release not only to the sufferer, but also to his attendants.

These symptoms manifest themselves in dogs in almost exactly the same way, there being three distinct stages. The dog becomes fidgety and nervous and behaves in a completely alien manner. The animal will be docile enough, but there will be something strange about its facial expression. It will lie as if watching some imaginary fly, and then leap forward, snapping and snarling, but in the early stages it rarely attacks man or beast.

The second stage is manifested by fits and fury, which eventually exhaust the animal until it collapses into the third stage of exhaustion, emaciation and paralysis of the hind quarters when it finally dies.

There is another form in animals known as dumb rabies when the lower jaw is paralysed, the animal loses its voice and can neither eat nor drink, but is generally quite passive, although the final stages are the same as in the furious form of the disease.

The disease is normally transmitted by saliva from an infected animal coming into contact with a wound or abrasion.

Up to 1885, although many people had been working to try to produce some sort of cure for this terrible disease, the only known treatment was that of cauterizing the wound and hoping for the best – hardly an adequate medical combination.

However, during that year, Louis Pasteur, working in his laboratory in Paris, produced the first form of treatment that offered any real hope of a cure.

In July 1885, a nine-year-old shepherd boy called Joseph Meister was brought to Paris to Pasteur's clinic. The poor child had been badly mauled by a rabid dog two days earlier, and although the wounds had been cauterized, as was then the common practice, Pasteur himself was certain that the boy would die. However, he decided to give the boy his treatment, and Joseph not only remained in perfect health, but he grew up to become concierge of the Pasteur Institute.

Pasteur's treatment was based on the fact that a virus capable of giving rabies by inoculation can be extracted from the tissues of a rabid animal, and then intensified or attenuated at will. The strength of the rabic virus, as determined by inoculation, is constant in the same species of animal, but is modified by passing through another species. For example: the natural virus of dogs is always of the same strength, but when it is inoculated into monkeys it becomes weakened. The process of attenuation can be carried on by passing the virus through a succession of monkeys until it loses the power of causing death. If this weakened virus is then passed back again through guinea-pigs, dogs or rabbits, its former strength is regained. If it is passed again through a succession of dogs, it then becomes intensified up to a maximum of strength, this being called the *virus fixe*.

Furthermore, Pasteur discovered that the strength can be modified by temperature and by keeping the dried tissues of a rabid animal containing the virus. Thus, if the spinal cord of a rabid dog was preserved in a dry state, which was done by drying the spinal cords in jars over caustic potash, the virus lost strength day by day.

Pasteur's system of treatment consisted of making an emulsion of these cords and graduating the strength of the dose by using a succession of cords, which had been kept for progressively diminishing lengths of time. Those that had been kept for fourteen days were used first, thus yielding virus of a minimum strength. This was followed by injections of diminishing age and increasing strength day by day for eleven days. After that, a return was made to a five-day emulsion, then four-day, finishing up with a second injection of the three-day, which was the maximum strength emulsion used.

In 1886 out of more than 2,500 patients thus treated, only twenty-five eventually died. In 1905, out of 727 patients injected, only four died, this showing an improvement in the mortality rate of almost 100 per cent.

For many years now efforts have been directed to the development of improved vaccines, the original Pasteur vaccine being followed by the production of dead vaccines, among them being the Semple phenolized fixed vaccine produced in 1919. Later, living fixed virus vaccines were developed for use in human medicine.

Hyper-immune anti-serum has also been developed with a view to conferring passive immunity during the early period before the vaccine can become effective. The site of the injury is all-important, for the nearer to the head, the faster the disease develops, so the immediate use of the serum is of particular importance when somebody has been severely bitten on the face.

A major disadvantage of these vaccines produced from nerve tissue is the side effect of post vaccinal encephalitis, or inflammation of the brain with distressing results, so recent research has been made into the production of vaccines propagated on embryonated eggs, and this is the method commonly used nowadays.

The currently available inactivated duck-embryo rabies vaccine developed and widely used in the USA hardly ever **produces unpleasant or dangerous side effects, even though** the actual course of injections into the wall of the stomach is extremely unpleasant. However, vaccination does not automatically confer protection, as it can have the effect of lengthening the incubation period of the disease, and this is true of dogs as well as of man.

The imaginary symptoms can be just as terrifying as the real thing, and George Fleming, who was President of the Central Veterinary Medical Society in 1871, told a story of a judge who was certain that he was suffering from hydrophobia. The poor man produced all the classic symptoms which persisted for several weeks. It was only after he had been persuaded to read literature about the disease that he realized that had he really been suffering from the disease, he would have been dead long since. His symptoms then diminished and finally disappeared.

George Fleming told another and even stranger story, this time about a merchant from Montpellier who was bitten by a rabid dog. There were no apparent ill consequences at the time, and very shortly afterwards the man left France to spend the next ten years in Holland. Eventually he returned to his native town, where he learned that another man who had been bitten by that very same dog had developed the disease and died a few days afterwards. The merchant was literally shocked to death, for Fleming relates that he developed the symptoms of the disease almost immediately, and this time the symptoms were genuine. It has always been believed that the disease can lie dormant for years and that an emotional shock can cause it to appear, so that story would seem to lend credence to the belief.

Fleming was in fact a member of the Committee of the Dogs' Home for some years, and at one time he offered to resign on the grounds that having published an article defending vivisection, he had made himself an undesirable member. However, the matter was put to the vote, and Fleming remained on the Committee for several more years.

That we in this country are free of the shadow of this disease bears tribute to the success of the controls imposed by the Ministry of Agriculture which have been in effect since the beginning of this century. The necessity for such controls is dramatically shown by the fact that one dog illegally imported by a returning soldier in 1918 was responsible for an outbreak that caused 319 confirmed cases in dogs of the disease and took five years to stamp out.

There is no room for sentiment where rabies is concerned, and it is beyond question that nothing whatever can justify the complete relaxation of the quarantine laws. It has been proved that they are the only safe way to keep rabies out of the country, as well as easily the most economical. Quarantine, however distasteful to the few, is a small price to pay for continued freedom from this dreadful disease for the many.

10

Cats

What is not widely known is that the Home at Battersea is not only a refuge for dogs, but for cats as well; and, in fact, a variety of other creatures have also been received, including foxes, rabbits, pigeons and parrots.

In 1882 the Committee decided to make provision for the many starving cats that roamed the streets, and three years later, thanks to the benevolence of a Mr Barlow Kennet, a start was made on the building of a cats' home to be known as the Whittington Lodge – a connotation that is easily understood.

Cats, mystical and sublime to those of us who come under their spell, evil and repellent to those unhappy mortals who have not seen the brilliant light that shines from their wide unwinking gaze, have been more venerated and perhaps more abused than any other living species. Macabre stories are told of the burning of cats for sacrifice in the Middle Ages to rid communities of spells said to have been cast over them by witches. The cats that were thus burnt were not seen as animals, but as creatures into whom the spirits of the evil and much-feared witches had entered, and that must therefore be destroyed.

The cat has long been associated with fire. 'The cat sat on the mat' does not present a complete mental picture, unless the mat is in fact in front of a blazing fire. In its role as guardian of the hearth the cat has been thought to protect houses from destruction by flames.

At times the cat forms a bridge between good and evil, and

at Aix-en-Provence in medieval times at the feast of Corpus Christi, a tom-cat was wrapped in swaddling clothes, placed in a shrine and worshipped as the incarnation of the god of sun. At noon, the unfortunate animal's time of veneration ended, as it was thrown alive into a bonfire in the city square, while anthems were sung by priests in solemn procession.

Although no traces of cats can be found by archaeologists in Palaeolithic times, nor in the rubbish-dumps of the small Neolithic cultures of Northern Europe, where the fragments of shellfish shells and broken tools are found mixed up in profusion with the bones of deer, wild boars, dogs and birds, there were certainly cats in the service of man as early as the Fifth Dynasty (*c.* 2,600 BC) in Egypt, where the veneration of the cat was carried to orgiastic extremes. The cat-goddess, Bastet, was first worshipped as a form of the sun, the giver and sustainer of life itself, and from the cat's identification with the sun comes the origin of the name of games played all over the world with string. African tribes make these 'cats cradles' to protect them from the never-ceasing blaze of the sun overhead, while Eskimos play their games with string in the hope of retaining the sun a few more days before their long period of winter darkness.

The Egyptians had a more practical side to their veneration of the cat, for with their acute powers of observation, and patience, combined with a natural way with animals, they not only succeeded in taming their new domestic animal, but they managed to train it to kill rats and mice, and also to catch and retrieve birds.

But the training of the cat has almost always had to be limited to the elementary process of house-training, and this is a task in fact that is generally undertaken by the mother cat. The cat views with disdain any attempt to make it perform – unless it chooses to put on a show of its own accord, which it often does at sun-down – but there are, of course, exceptions to this rule.

In the early 1930s nine tabby cats ended up at Battersea, presumably on the death of their owner, which had performed as a troupe all over the country. These feline clowns were full of tricks; one could walk a tight-rope the right way up, another clinging on from underneath. A third would lie quietly in a pram while taken for an outing by the fourth, and the highlight of the show these nine performers put on was a high dive by one of the clever little creatures from a spring-board down to a padded mat below. It is happy to relate that all nine were found good homes where their new owners must have been greatly entertained by their ingenious tricks.

The cat appears time and time again in the history of Arabia, one of the most famous stories being that of Mohammed's favourite pet, a cat called Muezza. On finding her curled up fast asleep on his sleeve when it was time for him to leave, the prophet preferred to cut the material from round the little animal rather than disturb her slumbers. When he returned, it is said, Muezza bowed to thank him, and Mohammed stroked her back three times from ears to tail, thus endowing her and all cats evermore with their well-known (but alas not infallible) ability to fall on their feet from a great height. Even since then, the Moslems have had nothing but indulgence for the cat, though the dog is conspicuous by his absence from their lore, being considered an unclean animal.

A Moslem diplomat tells a delightful story of his stay at Windsor as the guest of our present Queen. On the first day of his visit, one of the royal dogs made overtures of friendliness and licked him on the nose. His Excellency was covered with confusion, for as a good Moslem it was imperative that a liberal application of clay should immediately be put on the affected part. However, in his position as a royal guest, he found a dearth of the necessary substance, as he felt that the sight of an ambassador poking about in the rose beds, and then appearing with a nose adorned with earth might give rise to critical comment. The application had therefore to wait until the following day, when he arrived at a hotel in the north of England, and was able to make a stealthy visit to the garden under cover of darkness, where at last he was able to cleanse himself in the accepted way, according to his religion.

The cat was well known and loved in the Orient long ago, where India was the first to introduce the cat into one of her religions, for orthodox Hindu rites have for centuries required each of the faithful to feed at least one cat under his roof. It was the custom to keep cats in the Buddhist temple of Japan to protect the priceless manuscripts against the ravages of mice, and as Japan has always been famed as the country of the silkworms, it was inevitable that cats should also have been called up to protect these valuable creatures that endowed Japan's traditional industry, for a silkworm is a tasty titbit for mice. Japanese temples now are ornamented by strings of paper birds which represent the wishes for departed cats made by their erstwhile owners.

The cat in the form of a lion played a particularly important part in Lamaist Buddhism, for it was commonly believed that a lion walked into hell with Buddha, this story being echoed in other religions. However, in Tibet, dogs played the part of the non-existent lions, and it was thought that the lion had Gulliver-like qualities and could grow and diminish at will, thus enabling the Buddhist priests to identify their small dogs with the sacred beast.

We know that the cat has been used as a religious symbol for many centuries, but we are also equally aware that cats had an important part to play in the cult of diabolism, witness the black cat that has been associated with the witch from time immemorial. Poor black cat – so frequently an object of abuse, for the early Christians thought it to be the messenger of Lucifer, and this poor defenceless animal was sometimes sacrificed to quieten the fear they had of the devil. In the Middle Ages, a poor old woman was often accused of witchcraft and condemned to die a hideous death merely because, in common with many elderly people nowadays, she kept a cat for company and comfort.

The white cat has fared better on the whole. When a new

king of Siam was crowned in 1926, a white cat was carried in
the solemn procession to the enthronement. This cat was
presumably thought to have received the soul of the dead
king, for in ancient times when a member of the Siamese
royal family died, one of his cats would be entombed with
him. When the cat eventually escaped through one of the
small holes specially pierced in the roof of the tomb, then
the soul of the departed was thought to have passed into the
cat, which was taken to the temple and revered.

Cats are often thought to bring good luck, and this fact
was used to advantage by a British colonel in Burma during
the Second World War. On learning that in that country the
white cat was venerated as the symbol of good fortune, this
sagacious soldier had silhouettes of white cats stencilled on
every possible army vehicle, thus giving the impression that
the white cat was the emblem of the British Army. He also
sent out his men to collect large numbers of white cats, and
these animals were housed at British aerodromes. The rumour
spread swiftly round the superstitious native villages that the
aerodromes were invincible and unassailable, being the
refuge of hordes of these white harbingers of good fortune.
From that moment the local population stopped listening to
the Japanese propaganda that had been undermining all the
attempts of the British to construct strategic roads. The
Burmese peasant became dedicated to hard labour for the
Allied cause and the roads were built.

There are many versions of the Dick Whittington story,
whereby a cat by its ratting prowess brought wealth to its
downtrodden young owner, and Dick Whittington himself
won fame by becoming Lord Mayor of London three times, in
1397, 1406 and 1409. Versions of that story were doing the
rounds of the Persian markets a hundred years before it entertained its audiences in this country, and the same legend in
slightly different form was told in Italy, and again in Den-
mark, that home of fairytales and phantasy.

It is not surprising that the cat, like the dog, has found its
way into art all over the world. It is extravagantly depicted

in the works of Ancient Egypt, and also those of China and Japan. Artists in Europe from Leonardo da Vinci to Picasso have made use of the cat as a model, and there are many pictures in the galleries of Europe and America that depict the elegance, grace and mystery of the cat. One of the marked features of this pictorial history is that we are able to see how little the cat has changed in form from the very earliest times.

Many famous people have been addicted to cats, including such statesmen as Abraham Lincoln, Georges Clemenceau and Lord Chesterfield, who left a pension to his cat. Winston Churchill's favourite was present at many wartime cabinet meetings, while Theodore Roosevelt had two cats, Slippers and Tom Quartz, who reigned supreme at the White House.

Pasteur, Einstein and Schweitzer found relaxation in the company of their feline friends, and cats have long been recognized as the familiars of writers, giving purring encouragement both in the garrets of poverty and in the temples of fame.

Samuel Johnson defined the cat in his famous dictionary: 'A domestick animal that catches mice, commonly recognized by naturalists as the lowest order of the leonine species.' However, Boswell later was to record that Dr Johnson had a cat called Hodge so beloved by its master that, when the cat grew old, Dr Johnson fed it on a diet of oysters which he fetched himself daily, opening them and feeding them to his pet one by one. Boswell wrote:

I never shall forget the indulgence with which Dr Johnson treated Hodge, his cat: ... I am unluckily one of those who have an antipathy to a cat, so that I am uneasy when I am in a room with one, and I own I frequently suffered a good deal from the presence of the same Hodge.

I recollect him one day scrambling up Dr Johnson's breast, apparently with much satisfaction, while my friend, smiling and half-whistling, rubbed down his back and pulled him by the tail.

Writers of the calibre of Robert Southey, Horace Walpole, Alexandre Dumas, Leigh Hunt and Thomas Hardy shared an addiction for the animal; Charles Dickens told a story of a cat he once had that would snuff the candle while he was writing to persuade him to stop working and give it the attention it craved.

Colette, the immortal novelist, considered herself to be almost part cat, so much did she love the animals, her own never leaving her side, and Jean Cocteau is said to have become infected with her enthusiasm.

There are many varieties of cat that have been bred over the last fifty years or so for the specific purpose of gracing the show-bench, and this has given us for our pleasure some of the most beautiful animals in the world.

However, here we are concerned with what is commonly described as 'the alley cat', and in particular those without a hearth and home to grace. It is estimated that there are nearly half a million homeless cats in Paris, while in Italy there are thought to be more than a million and a half. Such estimates can only be arrived at by guess-work, but even so, we must be thankful that the numbers in this country are surely far, far less. The average number received each year at Battersea during the last decade is about a thousand, and happy to say, most of these are found good homes.

A new cat house was opened in 1970 as part of the first stage of the rebuilding operations, but Whittington Lodge still exists, though used for a different purpose. This new cat house is the last word in feline luxury, and is proving a great success in terms of good health for its inhabitants, who, when leaving Battersea to take possession of their new homes, give the impression of being from a race of super-cats.[1]

---

[1] I write from personal experience, my Battersea cat, Aurora – known in the family as the Tabby Tornado – being full of boundless energy and enthusiasm. She came to Scotland with us when she was about two months old and proved that Turkish swimming-cats are not a myth, by taking to the water with enthusiasm.

I I

Merciful Release

There are many distressing aspects that have to be touched upon when writing a history of the Dogs' Home at Battersea, and one of these is the subject of the methods of disposal of those poor animals that remain too sick and diseased for there to be a hope of finding a home for them after their statutory seven days in the Home.

In the early days the method of dispatch was by means of a drop or two of prussic acid placed on the tongue of the animal. But this method, while proving a quick and effective way of putting a dog out of its misery, had a great many drawbacks, not the least being the danger to the man administering the lethal dose. He ran a great risk, not only in handling the deadly poison, but he was also liable to have his hand bitten to the bone. At the time of the great rabies scare this was a danger indeed.

In 1882 a sub-committee was set up for the purpose of looking into possible extensions and improvements to the Home as a whole, and among their recommendations was the provision of a chamber for the destruction of both dogs and cats, particularly for cats. This was no doubt because although the administration of the death-dealing drops was a hazardous enough operation when dealing with dogs, it was doubly so when faced with a cat's sharp claws and needle-like teeth. The dogs were always found to be far more passive subjects, and the men who carried out the unenviable task developed an amazing degree of dexterity.

It was pointed out that prussic acid, although acting almost

F

instantaneously, did not by any means provide a painless death, and the Committee had heard that death chambers were being used in the United States of America with a considerable amount of success. Strangely enough, both the *Daily Telegraph* and the *Pall Mall Gazette* carried articles on the same date, 7 December 1882, suggesting that such a lethal chamber was a necessary addition to the Home, equally on grounds of utility and of humanity.

In 1883 Mr Richard Barlow Kennet who had already provided the wherewithal for Whittington Lodge, the cat house, offered to pay the costs of a lethal chamber, and its building was put in hand almost immediately.

Dr Benjamin Ward Richardson, FRS, as far back as 1869 had placed before the RSPCA a means for causing painless death by a narcotic. Twenty years earlier when he was still a student at St Andrews University, Benjamin Richardson began to experiment with the common puff-ball which in burning produces a smoke that causes narcotism in animals, and was often used by country people to stupefy bees in order to take away their honey. At about that time he assisted at an operation when the patient all but died under the chloroform, and as he watched her almost drifting away the thought first occurred to him that this would be the perfect way to destroy domestic animals – no pain, no fuss, no need to resort to the old methods such as hanging, drowning, shooting or stunning – just quiet oblivion. His subsequent researches into anaesthetics led him further, and to illustrate the fact that this would be a practical method, he set up a lethal chamber in his garden at Mortlake, to which neighbours brought their elderly pets to be, quite literally, 'put to sleep'.

The principle on which the lethal chamber at Battersea, designed by Dr Richardson, was built was that on entering it the animals would immediately be destroyed by carbonic-acid gas through which chloroform was introduced in the form of a spray. Death caused by this means would be similar to that in vogue at the time in left-bank Paris, where would-be suicides shut themselves up in an airtight room, and then lit a charcoal fire before taking their last sleep.

There was a long cage on wheels into which anything from ten to fifty dogs could be put at any one time, the general idea being that the dogs could be persuaded to walk quietly into the tray, which would then be pushed on rails into the lethal chamber, an anaesthetic sleep being induced within a minute and death taking place a couple of minutes later. This cage avoided the handling of the dogs, and was not withdrawn for a further thirty minutes. Death was thus caused by anaesthesia, and not, as many people thought, by suffocation or asphyxia.

Although the animals did sleep into death with no sign of a spasm or struggle ever being shown in their dead bodies on the removal of the cage, a contemporary journalist wrote a vivid description of that tray being rolled into the death chamber:

There was a silence of about a minute, after which began a strange unearthly wailing cry—just like the sound of some discordant crowd heard in the far distance. It would be easy to convince yourself that it is a cry of anguish and despair and piteous suffering. The fact is, however, that chloroform is an important element of the air of the chamber, and the dogs are just falling under the influence of it. Medical men recognise in this doleful wailing cry merely the same effect that chloroform always has upon human beings.... There is a steady crescendo and then an equally steady diminuendo, and in about another minute all is over. Doggie's troubles are all at an end, and his faithless friends are all forgotten. The biter and the bitten are slumbering side by side in peace and amity never to be broken again.

An extract from an article by Bulwer Lytton written at about the same time serves to lighten the gloom of that vivid and tragic description:

A waggish visitor the other day standing with a friend behind the cage containing the dogs and cats about to be sent into their last long sleep, playfully remarked that it would be well if some of our criminals and dangerous and incurable madmen could be sent shuffling off this mortal coil in a similar sensible and painless manner. 'Criminals and madmen' exclaimed his friend with a laugh that a certain well-known novelist would undoubtedly have called 'metallic', 'say, rather, our labour leaders, land agitators, our women who did, and women who could, our new woman and our bad musicians. Well might they be shuffled off, and nobody would feel one penny the worse. . . .'

Of course, no animal can be destroyed without the subsequent disposal of its carcase, so in 1886 the Committee were obliged to enter into a contract for the building of a crematorium at the Home, and this was completed at a cost of £700 and put into immediate use. Hitherto the bodies had been deposited at a farm at Enfield and subsequently used for manure, but the neighbours were beginning to complain, and so the farmer had refused to receive the carcases any longer.

The Secretary of the Home, Charles Colam, wrote to Sir Henry Ponsonby,[1] as the Committee felt that the Queen should be told of the proposed crematorium, and the Secretary's father, John Colam, also wrote from the RSPCA:[2] 'The matter of the Crematorium is a necessity. The sanitary authorities object to our using the bodies as heretofore. . . . In Germany they burn the bodies, first of all taking their skins to make gloves for the soldiers and then extracting the fat for medicinal purposes! We shall do neither;[3] but we are driven to the Crematorium. . . .'

John Colam, the father, received a terse reply from Sir Henry:[4] 'I have to thank you for all the documents you have been kind enough to send and which the Queen was very glad to receive. She is decidedly opposed to burning the bodies of dogs, but on this I will write to you soon.'

Sir Henry did in fact write to Charles Colam, the Secretary,

[1] RA P.P. 1/6 38
[2] RA P.P. 1/6 39
[3] The carcases are, in fact, taken from the Home nowadays and used for purposes of this sort.
[4] RA P.P. 1/6 40

at Battersea the following day with what was intended to be a helpful suggestion.[1] 'I have shown your letter[2] to the Queen but Her Majesty does not at all like the proposal of burning the bodies, and is informed that quicklime thrown over the body when it is buried prevents any evil consequence.'

Poor Charles Colam! The last thing he wanted to do was to offend his monarch, and it was almost impossible to explain that her suggestion was impractical in all the circumstances without incurring that risk. He wrote a conciliatory letter[3] to Sir Henry in which he pointed out not only the difficulty of finding a suitable burial ground, but also the fact that great expense would be incurred in digging holes for the bodies. He went on to say, most sensibly, that the Committee considered they would not be acting rightly if they spent their money just then in any work that was not of the nature of a permanency.

The Queen doubtless felt that if dogs could not be given a decent Christian burial, they should at least receive the next best thing. She told Sir Henry Ponsonby what she thought, and his reply to Colam's letter was both brief and to the point:[4]

Balmoral
August 27 1886

Dear Sir,

I showed your letter on the Crematorium to H.M. It does not change the Queen's opinion.

H.M. does not of course object to such an arrangement being effected but she will not contribute to it.

Henry Ponsonby

In 1904 a new lethal chamber was designed for the Home by Mr Bertram Richardson, the son of Sir Benjamin Ward Richardson, who had been knighted for his medical services.

[1] RA P.P. 1/6 41
[2] RA P.P. 1/6 38
[3] RA P.P. 1/6 42
[4] RA P.P. 1/6 43

The new chamber consisted of a glass and wood house, that looked rather like a conservatory, the object being to place the animals in a light room so that they would be less likely to be frightened. The majority of dogs that came into the Home in those days were terriers, unlike today, when a quick glance round at the inhabitants shows the predominant strain to be alsatian and various large cross-breeds based on that stock. So that first lethal chamber was designed to take about forty small dogs.

In 1917 the subject of humane destruction was raised once more by a member of the Committee, Mrs Edith Ward, who said that she had heard that electrocution was being used elsewhere. The Chairman, Mr Henry Selby, confirmed that this was so, and said that he was in fact also chairman of the institution at present using this method. He added that when some improvements had been made, the Dogs' Home were going to buy such an instrument of destruction.

However, the matter seems to have been put in abeyance, for there is no further mention of it until 1921, when another member of the Committee, Colonel Leonard Noble, again asked what was considered to be the most humane way of killing a dog.

He was told that the RSPCA had destroyed more than 40,000 cats by electrocution during 1920, the cats being put into a drawer, and when they were taken out again, they looked in death as if they had merely gone to sleep. However, practical difficulties had arisen with dogs, as with their harder and more horny paws it was difficult to make the correct contact. A man in America had designed a machine expressly to overcome this difficulty, and the RSPCA had invested £100 in it, only to find it a failure. One of the outstanding problems was the fact that whereas cats vary very little in size and weight, the range of size in dogs varies between the tiny pomeranian and the huge St Bernard, thus necessitating different voltages in each case. This is precisely the same thing that makes cat breeding so relatively easy, and dog breeding and parturition more complicated.

However, in 1934 a successful method was evolved that overcame all the difficulties. A commission had recently been formed to investigate the whole question of animal euthanasia composed of a group of man learned in veterinary matters, and this body expressed itself completely satisfied on every score with the new machine. So a unit was installed in the Dogs' Home at Battersea.

The great advantage of the method from the humane point of view was that each animal was dealt with individually, and it was not therefore necessary for them to witness one another's destruction. They therefore showed no fear of what was going to happen to them when it was their turn to enter the unit.

A new electric lethal chamber was put in in 1954 which had the full approval of the British Veterinary Association, and this electrothanator unit has been in use ever since. With certain modifications that have been carried out from time to time, it remains the most up to date method of dealing with the unpleasant but tragically necessary task.

12

A Country Annexe

In 1895, thirty-five years after the Home's inception, nearly 25,000 dogs were received during the year, which made a total of 63,651 over the past three years and the numbers of visitors to the Home had swelled to 60,000 per annum.

These astonishing figures gave the Committee of the Home food for thought. Perhaps it was time that a country home should be provided for those animals that were fortunate enough to remain in good health after their five days at Battersea?

Such an annexe would be, in effect, a convalescent home and would give the dogs a degree of liberty and individual attention that was out of the question in the confined space available at Battersea. It was hoped that the condition of the animals would improve, and that as a consequence they would command higher prices subsequently when the time came for them to be sold.

The Committee, headed by Sir George Measom, also Chairman of the Cancer Hospital and a well-known and successful writer of adventure books for boys, was composed of a good many influential people – a prominent member was the Rt Hon. Evelyn Ashley, son of that great philanthropist the seventh Earl of Shaftesbury,[1] and himself private secre-

[1] There is a memorial inscription at Harrow School which appears to have inspired the whole family :
'Near this spot Anthony Ashley Cooper afterwards 7th Earl of Shaftsbury while yet a boy at Harrow School saw with shame and indignation the pauper's funeral which helped to awaken his lifelong devotion to the service of the poor and the oppressed. Blessed is he that considereth the poor.'

A typical 'Battersea' collection of dogs – a picture that could have been taken at any time during the history of the Home

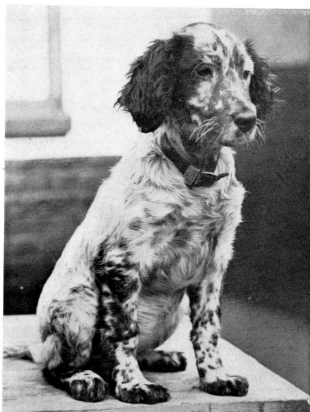

The two-millionth dog

Marking in

Waiting to be claimed

Who was it who
threw this puppy
out to die?

The devotion of
the keepers to
their charges has
always been a
marked feature of
the Dogs' Home.
It would seem
that the affection
is mutual . . .

'I'm here to stay'. This is Whisky the cat that adopted the Home

1969: Suzie is one of the two dogs who live permanently in Battersea Dogs' Home. Here she is receiving her check-up in the new clinic

Hundreds and thousands of dogs

Opposite: Anxious faces watching to see if this is their master coming to claim them at last

Their new friend

tary to Palmerston and Secretary to the Board of Trade from 180-2 – and there were such people as R. D'Oyly Carte, the Rev. George Townshend Driffield (a cousin of Lord Towns-hend), Miss Fay Lankester, Lady Dorothy Neville and Pro-fessor Pritchard.

The more business-minded members of the Committee pressed for a plan to be included whereby canine boarders could be taken at such a country Home. They felt, quite rightly, that canine paying guests would provide a constant and regular source of income to offset the large sum of capital that would be needed to launch such a project.

Local enquiries in Battersea were made first, as it was felt that perhaps an extension of the existing Home might suit the purpose equally well, but when it was found that land nearby was fetching £7,500 an acre, the idea was dropped abruptly.

It says a lot for the drive and enthusiasm of a small sub-committee set up for the purpose of finding a suitable site and consisting of Sir George Measom, Lt Col Parr and Mr John Colam (still the Secretary of the RSPCA), that they were able to announce the following year that their search had been successful. They had found about eight acres of land adjoining Hackbridge Station, which is on the London to Brighton railway line and only twenty-five minutes by rail from Victoria – a time that has not been improved on in more than seventy years – and eight miles by road from Batter-sea. The sum of £3,500 was being asked for this land, so the Committee appealed with enthusiasm for the necessary funds. Money poured in, an anonymous donation of £1,000 being received the day after the announcement that the land was available, and another £1,000 a few days later from a Mrs Grove-Grady, who had contributed £200 to the Home only a few days before.

The new Home, which had been built for £1,694, was opened with a grand ceremony on Saturday, 29 October 1898, when some two hundred people crowded into a marquee to hear the President, the Duke of Portland, give a brief outline of the history of the Dogs' Home up to that date, and then to declare the new buildings officially open. The Duke's speech was followed by a charming little presentation when one of the Battersea inmates, a wire-haired fox-terrier bitch, was given to the Duchess, no doubt intended for her two young children. After a sumptuous luncheon the whole assembly made a tour of the new premises, clutching their hats and their umbrellas against the onslaught of the typical late October weather.

There were sixteen kennels, each of which had a separate open court, and from these courts the dogs could be let out to the exercising fields at regular intervals. The floors throughout were made of portland cement, and each kennel was fitted with a removable wooden bench. The occasion was described vividly by the local journalist, who added that the keepers' lodge had a garden for the cultivation of green food for the inmates of the Home. Such green-stuff must have been very well disguised, for most dogs in my experience eagerly pick out every scrap of meat from a plate, leaving anything else in a tidy pile at the side.

The dogs were transported from Battersea in an ingeniously constructed van designed by Mr Henry Ward, who had succeeded Charles Colam as Secretary of the Home on Colam's death in 1893. It contained sixteen boxes and was so designed that no dog came into contact with any of the others, rather on the lines of the vehicles used by the police nowadays for the transport of their dogs.

Henry Ward was Secretary of the Home from 1893 to 1909. At the end of the January meeting of the Committee in 1909 he was presented with a handsome testimonial subscribed for by the President, the Duke of Portland, and by past and present members of the Committee. The minutes record: 'This testimonial took the form of a tray in Sheffield plate, engraved with a suitable inscription, including the names of the subscribers, and there were also a tea and coffee service *en suite*. It was a moving little ceremony, and Mr Ward had a little difficulty in returning thanks.'

A few days later, what was to prove an even more moving ceremony took place, for the combined staff of the Battersea and Hackbridge Homes gave, entirely at their own expense, a supper and concert at which Mr Ward was the principal guest of the evening.

The head keeper, Mr Dopson, took the chair, as his long service of more than thirty years gave him the right. Mr Ward was to receive another presentation, and this time it was a large and handsomely framed photograph of the staff, together with a a 'smoker's companion' subscribed for by all those present, and destined to stand in his study.

The scene in the local pub is easy to imagine. No doubt there was steak and pudding, with plenty of beer to swill it down, and then the concert afterwards must have been memorable, with no ladies and none of the Committee to cramp their style. The evening ended with the linking of arms and the singing of *Auld Lang Syne*, plenty of regrets, but plenty of laughter to chase away the tears.

The new country Home flourished, and was visited daily by Mr A. J. Sewell, veterinary surgeon to Queen Victoria, who had offered his services to the Home at Battersea completely free of charge in 1884. With a thriving practice in London, Mr Sewell also conducted his own boarding kennels at nearby Beddington, kennels that were bought by Spratts just before the First World War.

A number of healthy dogs were taken as boarders at Hackbridge which, while proving extremely profitable, also formed the thin end of the wedge, for the new Home had been started with a view to providing convalescents at Battersea with a happy place in which to recover their health and strength. It was with this end in sight that the Committee had waxed so enthusiastic over the whole idea. In 1910 an arrangement was made with the Board of Agriculture and Fisheries whereby a limited number of dogs were taken in at Battersea for quarantine under the Importation of Dogs Order of 1901. This was when the paying boarders began to oust the Battersea strays, and the Home was run on very different lines from those originally envisaged.

The fees for the boarding of the quarantine dogs ranged from three shillings to ten shillings a week, and this included veterinary attendance, but not medicines. The fond owners were allowed to visit their pets at any time of day during business hours.

In 1914 the great event at Hackbridge was the arrival of the sledge dogs that had been collected by Sir Ernest Shackleton for his imperial trans-Antarctic expedition. These dogs, however, are of such interest that they merit a chapter on their own.

Sad to relate, Hackbridge had to be closed at the busiest time of the war, owing to an outbreak of distemper that ran through the place, brought in by dogs picked up by the troops in France, and sent home to Hackbridge to serve their quarantine period.

In 1920 what was perhaps to be the most famous visitor of all came to board at Hackbridge. This was a St Bernard called Riffel that was the property of Mr Lloyd George.

Lloyd George's snap election held at the end of the war was intended to result in a stupendous vote of confidence in his party as being the one that had won the war, and it did in fact result in a resounding victory for the Prime Minister. But it hardly reflected the feelings of the nation, as half the voting population had not yet returned from the army, and although many of them had arrived at the age of franchise while serving under the colours, they had not yet had an opportunity to get their names on the electoral registers. Most of Lloyd George's nominees were returned almost unopposed in what must have been one of the most apathetic elections in history – one that did not even merit a mention in a collection of contemporary reports produced by the *Daily Telegraph* covering that period that they published in 1955 at the time of the newspaper's centenary. Lloyd George, known as 'the Wizard of Wales', had been expected to produce a halcyon postwar new world overnight with a wave of his magic wand.

However, prime ministers are always newsworthy, and it is reported that when Mr Lloyd George went on an autumn holiday in 1920, he did not return alone. He was accompanied by a large and exuberant young St Bernard dog that he had bought, perhaps rather misguidedly, from a Swiss peasant. On his arrival in this country the Prime Minister was advised to send the dog to Hackbridge where it could spend its six months' quarantine. Riffel was followed hotfoot by the Press, and one journalist commented that the animal looked quite capable of bringing its master back to Downing Street should he show any signs of straying.

When Riffel's stay at Hackbridge ended he was taken to No. 10 Downing Street *en route* for Chequers, and while the dog was there, a reporter from the *Star*, evening off-shoot of the Liberal newspaper, the *News Chronicle*, visited him. This young reporter's description of the visit is a masterpiece of contemporary journalism:

When I called to see Riffel this morning, I was taken into the garden and told to wait. 'And if I were you,' said the dog's personal attendant, 'I should lean against the wall. He's rather an affection-ate creature is Riffel.'

From the subterranean parts of the house came a muffled roar that grew and grew until it sounded like the cough of a croupy mastodon, a deep throated 'Woof!' that made the windows (and the *Star* man) shake. Then a soft, sloppy, pitter patter in the passage, such as an elephant might make, and Riffel bounded into the garden, leaped seven feet into the air and nearly knocked a tree down. Then he saw me, and stopped, and looked and listened, hanging out a steaming tongue like a pound of liver. 'Hallo!' he said. 'What's this? A reporter? I've never tasted one of those. Are they good to eat?'

He strolled slowly across to me, stood up, put his fore feet on my shoulders, and looked long and earnestly into my face. Evidently he liked what he saw, for he put out some more of his tongue and kissed me heartily on both cheeks.

'Gentle as a lamb!' said Riffel's attendant, 'and as playful as a —as a pachyderm. I take him—I mean, he takes me—for a walk in the park every morning, and it's splendid exercise. I can do the half mile in about forty seconds now, with hurdles!'

According to his official description, Riffel is a pure-bred St Bernard, straight from the Alps, where Mr Lloyd George bought him from a shepherd. Maybe there is a strain of the brontosaurus in him, a dash of kangaroo, and a soupçon of the buffalo; but in the main he is St Bernard all right. You could see he was trained in the mountains by the way he leaped about the garden, vaulting over imaginary glaciers, springing from peak to peak, and galumphing from one Alp to another. Twice he got it into his head that I was a traveller lost in the snow, and proceeded to rescue me by the trousers. The trouble with No. 10 is the shortage of Alps and avalanches for him to play with. There isn't room for both the Premier and Riffel at No. 10, so R.M.G. (That stands for Riffel Must Go). But there is no truth in the story that Mr Lloyd George is having Snowdon moved to Chequers to make his pet feel more at home.

'And what do you feed him on?' I asked his keeper.

'Bones and biscuits, mostly,' was the answer, 'but evidently we've under estimated his appetite, because he's eaten about six leather collars and leads since he came, and tasted several doormats.'

'And how about his politics?' I asked, 'Does he lick the hands of the Hard-faces or bite the Wee-Frees?'[1]

'Oh yes!' said his attendant, 'he's been well brought up. He knows his master's voice all right, and seems to recognise the Opposition Members every time. While, as for people of Liberal opinions—'

Riffel looked up, sniffed like a soda siphon, and opened his great mouth that steamed like washing day.

'He spots them a mile off. Grinds his teeth at them, and.... Not that way out, Sir! There's spikes on the top of that wall.... In here, quick! Never mind your hat, I'll send that on to you if he leaves any of it.'

By 1922, Hackbridge was proving a considerable financial asset to Battersea, largely due to the enormous numbers of dogs being brought back by the troops as they returned from active service or from the British Army of Occupation.

---

[1] The Wee-Frees were the few remaining supporters of Asquith.

A *Country Annexe*

In 1930 the premises had a face lift. The kennels were re-roofed and alterations were made to what had originally been intended as the keeper's lodge, but which had been occupied for many years by the resident veterinary surgeon, John Stow Young, who had joined the staff in 1910 when Hackbridge became a quarantine station. All the boundary fences were repaired, and more outside runs were provided for cats, making accommodation in all for 491 dogs and 155 cats, with an additional twenty-eight pens that could be used for either. A forge, a carpenters' shop and a paint shop were provided by the reconstruction of the service block in the main kennels. Most of the work was carried out by the staff.

In that year, 1930, Mr Guillum Scott spoke confidently at the Annual General Meeting about the future of Hackbridge, saying that it was very satisfactory to note how very many more people were beginning to appreciate the need for first-class boarding accommodation for their dogs. He also said that it was very largely due to John Stow Young's advice and suggestions that they had been able to carry out with such success the sometimes difficult work at Hackbridge, keeping the dogs in health and good condition, not only to the satisfaction of the owners, but in accordance with the stringent regulations laid down by the Ministry of Agriculture.

Only one year later, Mr Moss Blundell, who had been a member of the Committee at Battersea for twenty-four years, was to state that anything he had to say about Hackbridge might be regarded in the nature of a 'swan song'. He said that the Ministry of Agriculture had changed its policy and reverted to its old one of licensing dogs to the private premises of veterinary surgeons. As the Ministry itself had asked the Home to set up Hackbridge as a quarantine station, it would seem that Moss Blundell was not at all sure of his facts, and was speaking out of turn. The Ministry of Agriculture did in fact require a veterinary surgeon to visit quarantine kennels daily, a condition that is still imposed. But at no time has it ever required the kennels to be licensed under a veterinary surgeon.

The following year losses were cut at Hackbridge due to the reorganization of the management and work carried out there, but at the same time the Committee were told that their contracts in London with the police were due to be terminated by 31 December 1932. They were asked to tender for new services to be provided but, under a new contract, they would be required to open a new home somewhere on the north side of the Thames. The police felt that such a place would prove more convenient to people living on that side of the river.

This edict must have been received at about the same time that a firm offer for the purchase of the Hackbridge kennels, lock, stock and barrel, was received from Spratts, on behalf of one of their subsidiary companies, the Dogs' Sanatorium Ltd of Beddington Lane – the kennels from which Shackleton had transferred his huskies to the care of Hackbridge[1] and which were originally bought from A. J. Sewell by Spratts. A former offer from the Hackbridge Cable Company had been turned down, as it was for the site only.

Spratts were offering £10,000, and not only did they want to take over the premises, but they also wanted to take on the eight men employed as kennelmen and keepers. However, they were not prepared to take on John Stow Young, the veterinary surgeon, as they already employed a veterinary surgeon of their own. This was a Mr R. H. Clarke, who conducted the negotiations for the property on behalf of Spratts and had been running the Wallington kennels since before the war, when they were bought by the firm.

Captain Stow Young had joined the Army Veterinary Corps at the outbreak of the First World War, and he won the Military Cross for conspicuous bravery and devotion to duty near Guy. On 26 March 1918, while in charge of an Army Veterinary Corps party, he took over a large number of wounded horses that had stampeded under the heavy shell fire. Showing great coolness and courage, he calmed the frightened animals and restored order. He then placed

[1] See page 92.

wounded men on their backs, and in the face of an enemy advance he helped them all back to safety, bringing back their arms and equipment which would otherwise have had to be abandoned.

When Captain Stow Young had been told that the Hackbridge kennels were in danger of closure a year or two before they were in fact sold, he had offered to take them over himself and have them licensed by the Ministry of Agriculture under his name as a veterinary surgeon. He suggested that he should have them on a twenty-one-year lease at £600 per annum, and asked to be given first refusal on the property. It is very difficult to understand why, in the face of this good offer from a man they had every reason to trust, the Committee ignored it, and saw fit to sell the place to Spratts only a year later.

They were, of course, being pressed by the police to open a new home, and their chairman, Sir Charles Hardinge, had managed to find a suitable site at Bow – again between railway lines – so it may have been felt that a capital sum in the hand would be a better proposition at the time than the prospect of a regular income. The only opponents to the sale on the Committee then were Mr Burton and Major Mead, and they both died during the year, thus making the decision to sell unanimous. The Bow Home was opened that year.

Captain Stow Young was given a grant by the Committee and went into private practice in Wallington. He is spoken of with enthusiasm by Frank Beattie, MRCVS, who succeeded R. H. Clarke as Manager of the Wallington and Hackbridge kennels. Mr Beattie himself is now in private practice in Wallington, for Spratts sold the Hackbridge kennels in 1970. There is a touch of irony in the fact that they went to a cable company and the price reputed to have been paid for the site alone was in the region of £250,000. What a prize the Battersea Committee of 1934 let slip through their hands.

13
Shackleton

The freezing of the sea is like the closing of eyelids in sleep, a relaxed and languid calm in which the water seems to take on flesh, a rippling surface of skin, golden and glowing in the low autumn sun. The long-rolling limbs of the sea are still, and the passage of wind becomes soundless.

from *South* by Graham Billing[1]

The names of Cook, Scott, Nansen, Amundsen, Shackleton, Hillary and Fuchs will always live in the annals of exploration, but their names are bound up for ever with the magical and almost mystical spell cast in our minds by the frozen plateaux of the Antarctic.

Ernest Shackleton, destined to become one of the immortals, came from a family of professional men and landowners, not from a race of seafarers and adventurers. There was no family tradition to send him on his journeys that were to lead to fame and fortune, and finally to his death.

The son of Irish parents, he not only inherited a charm that is vividly remembered half a century after his death, but he also had more than his fair share of the gift of the gab, made all the more attractive by a touch of brogue, and a theatrical flair for putting himself across to his audience. He had a dynamic personality that inspired his men to follow wherever he chose to lead. At the time of writing, there are only a handful of survivors of his 1914-17 expedition still alive.

---

[1] Published in New Zealand in 1964 and in the United Kingdom in 1965 by Hodder and Stoughton ; not to be confused with the book of the same name by Shackleton.

One of them, Mr Walter How, one of Shackleton's most trusted men, at the age of eighty-six reiterates what he said in 1955 in a recorded conversation with Margery and James Fisher, whose book *Shackleton* he illustrated with skill and charm, being a talented amateur artist: 'If he had half a pipe of tobacco, he'd give you half of it, if there was no other to share out. And he'd never ask you to do something he wasn't prepared to do himself.' This, of course, was one of the secrets of Shackleton's leadership, this and an innate understanding and sympathy with his fellow men.

By nature a gambler and adventurer, perhaps if Shackleton had lived in an earlier age he would have been a buccaneer. In his all too short span of forty-eight years he crowded in more, far more, than his share of life and adventure. He brought to whatever he was doing an enthusiasm and freshness of interest that stimulated all concerned, and inspired them in their turn to catch at 'joy as it flies'.

He joined the Merchant Navy at sixteen, moving from ship to ship, and from line to line. Ten years later, with marriage in mind, he applied for a commission in the Royal Navy, but this was refused, a rebuff that was to rankle with him ever more. He then turned to journalism and became a sub-editor on Pearson's *Royal Magazine*. Shackleton was soon to realize that journalism does not follow a path that is liberally strewn with gold, so when he heard that the Royal Scottish Geographical Society was looking for a secretary, he sent in an application for the job. This he felt might lead to better things, and it did.

The year he spent with the Society has been described as 'a little alarming and sometimes stormy for the more conservative members of the Society's Council', and at the end of that first year Shackleton, and possibly the Council too, was ready for a change. He jumped with alacrity at the chance of standing as Liberal-Unionist candidate in 1906 for the carpet-bag constituency of Dundee. The Liberal-Unionists were a splinter group led by Joseph Chamberlain that had moved over to the Conservative side after the split in the Liberal Party over home rule for Ireland in 1886.

Although unsuccessful at the polls, Shackleton became enormously popular in the working-class districts, and his time was not wasted, for he met men with money and influence in the business world. He plunged into gamble after gamble with exuberant and reckless optimism. One of his contacts was William Beardmore, later Lord Invernairn, a Clydeside ship-builder and industrialist of enormous wealth, who later guaranteed the money for Shackleton's first Antarctic expedition in 1908.

When Shackleton returned from this expedition which succeeded in hoisting the Union Jack within a hundred miles of the South Pole, he found that he was received as a national hero. Captain Robert Falcon Scott was waiting for him at Charing Cross Station, for in spite of much gossip regarding their relationship, the two men, although indulging in healthy rivalry, were far too concerned with what they themselves were doing to brood and develop any ruthless ambition to outdo one another. With a cordial message from King Edward VII in his pocket Shackleton found himself immediately summoned to Downing Street, where Asquith had completed his first year as prime minister. Evidently political differences were overlooked, for Shackleton received the welcome news on this visit that the government would pay off the debts of the expedition.

In the years that were to lie between that first expedition and the one with which we are concerned, Shackleton, toiling to pay his debts, dreamed of making a fortune, and he also dreamed of the Antarctic, which had kept its hold on him.

It was with relief that he eventually turned his mind to the adaptation of a proposal that had been made by W. S. Bruce in 1908. This was to land a crossing party on the Weddell Sea coast which lies to the south of South America, with the landing of another support and depot-laying party in the Ross

90

Sea, north of Tasmania, with the object of a trans-Antarctic continental crossing.

From experience Shackleton had learned that sledges were best pulled by dogs. Ponies and tractors had been tried and found dismally lacking. Shackleton, although at first inclined to agree with Scott who had said: 'To my mind, no journey ever made with dogs can approach the height of the fine conception which is realised when a party of men go forth to face hardships, dangers and difficulties with their own un-aided efforts . . .', had a change of mind. This happened prob-ably as a result of Roald Amundsen's achievement of 1911-12 and after conversations with the Norwegian explorer. In December 1911, Amundsen had been the first man to plant a flag at the South Pole, and he always avowed that men alone were not enough for a long haul. He had found that a kind of mental lethargy set in after a length of time, which could prove acutely dangerous, and often had fatal results.

Shackleton also learned from Amundsen that it was no use relying on raw, untrained dogs that were liable to run amok and be more trouble than they were worth, so he enlisted the services of a well-known Canadian husky-handler to recruit a hundred dogs from the shores of Lake Winnipeg. The first part of his task performed, this husky-team trainer travelled to England in the steamer, *Montcalm,* which berthed at Mill-wall Docks on 5 July 1914, from which nearly a hundred crates were unloaded, each one containing a carefully selected dog for use on the expedition.

All the dogs were half-breeds, being husky-collie, husky-St Bernard and husky-wolf crosses – husky bitches are often tied to a tree at night in Canada in the hope that they will have a litter of puppies sired by a wolf, for this first cross gives added stamina to the breed. Huskies as a breed have a reputa-tion for extreme savagery, but this belief is unfounded by fact. When allowed to be domesticated they are excellent companions, and although inclined to be aloof and suspicious with strangers and savage with their own kind, they are good-natured and demonstrative with the people they know. When well-fed and cared for, they are lovable animals, and the dogs that were chosen for Shackleton's expedition were no exception to this rule, as is borne out by Walter How, who speaks of the dogs with affection and still remembers some of them individually more than fifty years later.

The huskies left the London docks in a fleet of horse-drawn vans that were boldly emblazoned with the words 'SPRATTS' on either side. Some of the dogs were bound for the Spratts' kennels at Beddington, but the majority were going to Hackbridge. Shackleton was not satisfied, however, with the Beddington accommodation, and a couple of weeks later, the whole party were to be found at Hackbridge where they drew large crowds of sight-seers, and where they were kept for two months completely free of charge.

Ernest Shackleton's proposed expedition was receiving not only publicity in plenty, but also a great deal of criticism. There was a strong body of opinion that felt that an expedition of such magnitude involving a number of men and a big sum of money should not be hazarded at such a time of national crisis.

Shackleton himself was worried stiff:

We sailed from London on Friday August 1 1914, and anchored off Southend all Saturday. On Sunday afternoon I took the ship off Margate, growing hourly more anxious as the ever-increasing rumours spread, and on Monday morning I went ashore and read in the morning paper the order for general mobilization.

It is typical of the man's character that he wasted no time but acted immediately. He wired the Admiralty offering the services of his men – fifty-six, chosen out of more than five thousand applications[1] – all his equipment, and the two ships, the *Aurora* then based in Australia, and his own ship, the *Endurance*. A signal was received in return which merely said 'Proceed', but two hours later, this terse message was

---

[1] These figures were given to me by Walter How, whose own application was successful because it was 'noted as among the lively applications, which are not many'.

followed by a wire from Winston Churchill, then First Lord of the Admiralty. Winston Churchill was the man who had boldly seen to it that for every one German keel laid down in the years immediately before 1914, two were laid down in British shipyards. He was more specific and thanked Shackleton for his offer, but instructed him to carry on with his plans, as the expedition was going with the full sanction of the Scientific and Geographical Societies. Shackleton himself said later that it was not as if they were off on a cruise of the Caribbean.

The original plan had been for the *Endurance* to sail to Cowes, and to lie at anchor there while King George V came aboard to inspect the ship and wish them all God-speed. Owing to the crisis, this plan had to be abandoned, and instead the King sent for Shackleton from Plymouth, giving him a Union Jack to carry on the voyage. Shackleton kept this Union Jack with the Bible that had been given to him by Queen Alexandra a few weeks earlier when she had visited the ship in dock. Later, when all personal possessions had perforce to be jettisoned, Shackleton tore out one page from this Bible and carried it with him. It was the page from *Job*, 38-29 which included these words:

> Out of whose womb came the ice? and the hoary
> frost of heaven, who hath gendered it?
> The waters are hid as with a stone, and the
> face of the deep is frozen.

That same day, at midnight, war was declared.

The dogs, that now numbered ninety-six, one having been destroyed at Shackleton's command, who thought it unfit for service in the conditions they would be meeting, left Hackbridge in two lots. Twenty-six of them left on 16 September bound for Tasmania to join the *Aurora*, whose crew were waiting to establish depots in the Ross Sea area. The other seventy went the following day to sail by mail-ship to Buenos Aires, being accompanied on the first leg of their long journey, from which none of them was destined to return, by one of the keepers from the Hackbridge home.

This keeper, George Wyndoe, had had a chequered career before he went to Hackbridge. He had made a precarious living by selling patent medicines at fairgrounds all over the British Isles, and had had to make many a hasty departure, when it was found that he had resorted to replenishing his scanty stocks with ordinary tap water. A man of amusing character, full of anecdotes, he stayed in the employ of the Dogs' Home until retirement, and Mr Jack Tyler, who did so much of the research for this book, remembers him well when he came to Battersea to collect his pension and to spin a yarn with his old friends.

Shackleton was well pleased with the way Wyndoe handled the dogs, and an example of the leader's thoughtfulness is shown by the fact that he sent a glowing testimonial to the Dogs' Home when he finally returned to this country himself in 1917. He glossed over the fact that Wyndoe's control cannot have been absolute, for Sally and Snapper became the proud parents of four puppies, Roger, Ruby, Nelson and Nell, during the journey to South Georgia.

One of the first setbacks experienced by the expedition was the non-appearance of the Canadian trainer, who had returned to Canada after bringing over the dogs and was due to meet the ship in Buenos Aires. No explanation was ever given for his defection, but one of the more serious consequences was that as he was to have been responsible for the general health and wellbeing of the dogs, when a severe epidemic of worms broke out it was found that the worm-powders had been left behind, and several of the valuable dogs were lost.

They had set sail from Buenos Aires on 26 October, 1914, but by 27 October the following year, things were looking black. The *Endurance* had been caught fast in the paralysing grip of pack-ice for the past four months, and on that date she had to be abandoned before she broke up completely, crushed like a matchboard model in the grip of a mighty vice.

From then on, their home had to be the ice floes. The dogs

had been moved off the ship some time before, and they were housed in what became known as 'dogloos', whose varying towers and minarets were objects of great pride to the men who had constructed them like children building sandcastles.

Morale was still high amongst men and dogs, and much training of the dog teams had been carried on while there was still hope that the *Endurance* would eventually be free of the ice, and able to continue her journey.

The dogs were divided into six teams of nine dogs apiece. They had a variety of names, many reflecting their characters, temperaments and countenances:

Songster	Martin	Chirgwin[1]
Sandy	Splitlip	Steamer
Mack	Sidelights	Peter
Mercury	Swanker	Fluffy
Wolf	Sammy	Steward
Amundsen	Sub	Slippery
Hercules	Bosun	Elliott
Samson	Luke	Roy
Caruso	Saint	Noel
Spotty	Satan	Shakespeare
Sadie	Chips	Jamie
Sue	Stumps	Bumner
Sally	Snapper	Smuts
Jasper	Painful	Spider
Tim	Bob	Lupoid
Sweep	Simeon	
Sailor	Soldier	

Rugby
Upton
Bristol
Millhill } These were named for schools and colleges that had supported the expedition.

Together men and dogs learned, the hard way and quickly. Shackleton described the dogs as 'big, sturdy animals, chosen for endurance and strength', but he added, 'If they are as keen

[1] Named after a music hall artist who blacked his face. One day he inadvertently rubbed one eye, and then became known as 'the white-eyed coon'.

to pull our sledges as they are now to fight one another all will be well.' Although the dogs were muzzled, they did not let this fact inhibit them, but fell on each other at every opportunity. However, this was not the whole picture, for the puppies were taken under the wing of one of the biggest dogs, appropriately named Amundsen. This tough dog 'fostered' the pups and played with them gently.

As their training progressed, the teams were able to enter into competition with each other, culminating in what was known as 'the Dog Derby'. Shackleton showed his wisdom by encouraging this rivalry among dog teams. The men had to be kept lively and alert, and what better way than by arranging a sporting event of this kind?

The teams were in splendid condition, the crowds were provided by curious penguins, two or three sailors made a book, cigarettes and chocolates being the favourite wagers, and excitement ran high. They were off. The course was run in two minutes sixteen seconds by Frank Wild's team, Wild being second-in-command. This was a popular victory, but Hurley, the photographer, challenged the winner to another race with passenger up the following day, and he won this race; though on a protest, as Wild's passenger, Shackleton himself was pitched off the sledge at the crucial moment that might have meant victory.

These were to be looked back on as halcyon days in the light of what was to follow, for at the end of March 1916, preparations had to be made for them all to leave in three boat parties in an attempt to reach Elephant Island.

The dogs had to be shot, and this was described as the worst job of all, coming as it did on the heels of disaster after disaster and many bitter tears were shed by the tough explorers. The dogs had been their friends and allies, and had provided the men with objects on which to lavish their affection and warmth of feeling, emotions which have to be kept strictly under control under such conditions of endurance and extreme hardship.

The last dogs went on 2 April, and their carcases were

dressed for food. They had to be, for sentiment is out of keeping with starvation. Some of the dog-meat was cooked, and
was found not at all bad. Mr How described it as better than
some of the meat he gets from his butcher nowadays; tough
but tasty.

The men from *Aurora* were having their difficulties too.
It had not been found possible to give any time to the training
of their dog teams, and they had to start on their journeys
straight away, raw men and dogs. The party reached the
agreed latitude on 20 February and they built the depot and a
line of cairns the following day. Then they had a desperate
return journey, all of them being appallingly frost-bitten, and
the dogs sharing in the hardships. The animals were so hungry
at times that they ate their harnesses and anything else they
could find lying about. One by one, they collapsed, just curl-
ing up in their tracks and dying – but not until they had saved
the lives of the party, for without those dogs the men would
never have returned.

Oscar, Con, Gunner and Towser, 'four faithful friends', went
for three days without any food, and yet they continued to
pull their loads willingly and with dogged determination;
what an almost unique opportunity to use that hackneyed
phrase with complete truth and aptness. Mackintosh, the
leader of the party, said, 'If ever dogs saved the lives of anyone, then they saved ours.'

Shackleton eventually succeeded in saving all but two of
his men, but the expedition as such was a failure. The journey
across the continent had hardly been begun. The scientific
results were very different from what had been hoped, and
the geological and biological collections lost altogether. Yet
Shackleton was to return to this country to find himself a
hero, for '. . . fighting against a simple adversary, fighting to
beat the Antarctic, he demonstrated, more clearly than anyone else in this sphere, the power of man's unconquerable
mind.'[1]

[1] James & Margery Fisher, *Shackleton*, (James Barrie, 1957).

14

Back to Battersea

Now we have to make a return, not only around the world, but also in time, for we left the fortunes of the Dogs' Home at Battersea at the turn of the century to divert to the founding of the new Home at Hackbridge.

One of the problems that becomes evident on an examination of the records is that of dog-stealing. The Home was still on good terms with the police, and in 1903 the chair at the Annual General Meeting was taken by the Commissioner of Metropolitan Police.

Before the police had reached the level where they commanded respect and trust, which they undoubtedly did by the end of the last century, they had undergone a somewhat chequered career. In 1822 a special commission had been formed to examine the problems of policing the country, and in 1829 Robert Peel and the Duke of Wellington were between them successful in nursing through Parliament a bill for police reform. This bill has had long-lasting effects for which we all have cause for gratitude.

The image of the police when they first appeared in the streets of London wearing their top hats and blue coats was very different to the one we know now. The 'Peelers' were greeted by mocking laughter or sullen hostility. However, gradually they won the respect of the populace, for the security of the man in the street was increased as crime diminished. Where London led, the rest of the country soon followed, for this new Metropolitan Police Force was found to be so vastly superior to its forerunners, the old watchmen, Bow Street runners, and the semi-military forces that had preceded them, that requests began to come in from all over the country asking for the loan of competent officers to help the counties to organize their own police forces.

Battersea, as we have heard, had always had a link with the police, and in 1906 the Dogs Act was passed and came into operation on 1 January 1907 with the following provisions:

1 Liability of owner of dog for injury to cattle.
2 Power of Board of Agriculture to make orders about dogs.
3 Seizure of stray dogs.
4 Notice to police of finding of stray dogs.
5 Exemption of sheep dogs, etc. from excise licence.
6 Burying of carcases.
7 Definition of cattle.
8 Application of Act to Scotland.
9 Application of Act to Ireland.
10 Repeal.
11 Short title and commencement.

The heading that particularly concerns us is No. 3:

1 Where a police officer has reason to believe that any dog found in a highway or place of public resort is a stray dog, he may seize the dog and may detain it until the owner has claimed it and paid all expenses incurred by reason of its detention.
2 Where any dog so seized wears a collar having inscribed thereon or attached thereto the address of any person, or the owner of the dog is known, the chief officer of police, or any person authorised by him in that behalf, shall serve on the person whose address is given on the collar, or on the owner, a notice in writing stating that the dog has been so seized, and will be liable to be sold or destroyed if not claimed within seven clear days after the service of the notice.
3 A notice under this section may be served either
   a by delivering it to the person on whom it is to be served; or
   b by leaving it at that person's usual abode or at the address given on the collar; or
   c by forwarding it by post in a prepaid letter addressed to

that person at his usual or last known place of abode, or at the address given on the collar.

4   Where any dog so seized has been detained for seven clear days after the seizure, or, in the case of such a notice as aforesaid having been served with respect to the dog, then for seven clear days after the service of the notice, and the owner has not claimed the dog and paid all expenses incurred by reason of its detention, the chief officer of police, *or any person authorised by him in that behalf*,[1] may cause the dog to be sold or destroyed in a manner to cause as little pain as possible.

5   *No dog so seized shall be given or sold for the purposes of vivisection.**

6   The chief officer of police of a police area shall keep, *or cause to be kept,** one or more registers of all dogs seized under this section in that area which are not transferred to an establishment for the reception of stray dogs. The register shall contain a brief description of the dog, the date of seizure, and particulars as to the manner in which the dog is disposed of, and every such register shall be open to inspection at all reasonable times by any member of the public on payment of a fee of one shilling.

7   The police shall not dispose of any dog seized under this section by transferring it to an establishment for the reception of stray dogs *unless a register is kept for that establishment** containing such particulars as to dogs received in the establishment as are above mentioned, and such register is open to inspection by the public on payment of a fee not exceeding one shilling.

8   The police officer *or other person** having charge of any dog detained under this section shall cause the dog to be properly fed and maintained.

9   All expenses incurred by the police under this section shall be defrayed out of the police fund, and any money received by the police under this section shall be paid to the account of the police fund.

Section 4 stated that any person taking possession of a stray dog should either return it to its owner straight away, or give notice in writing to the chief officer of police in the district

---

[1] The italicized sections are those that specifically concern the Dogs' Home.

where the dog was found, with a full description of the dog, where it was found, and where it was being kept. Anybody failing to comply with this provision would be liable to a fine. This section was levelled at the dog thief, though it is in fact open to misconstruction, for it was perfectly simple for a dog thief to convey to and report in one police division as 'found' any dog picked up anywhere else. Another dog could even be substituted for the one 'acquired'.

There was undoubtedly a considerable traffic of this kind, and there were cases too when an unscrupulous man would advertise for dogs, not pay for them, but dispose of them to hall porters, etc. of hospitals for vivisection. Few of the dogs returned as 'In possession of Finder 'ever met up with their owners again. What often happened was that an owner was sent to the address given them by the police and would be told either that the dog had died, run away, or that it had never been at that address.

The Home is fully and adequately covered by law, for once the statutory seven days have elapsed the dog becomes the sole property of the Home to dispose of as it sees fit, whether by finding it a new home, or whether by humane destruction.

If a dog has gone to a new owner and the first and indisputable owner turns up after a length of time has elapsed, it is the practice to write to the new owner without disclosing his address to the first one. All too often the new owner will refuse to part with his new pet, and there is nothing that can then be done.

In the same year that the Dogs Act came into effect, the Home rebuilt its kennels, the new buildings being designed by Clough Williams-Ellis of Port Meirion fame. Six of the arches were divided into pens, providing accommodation for 250 to 300 dogs. A seventh arch was used for storage as before, but there were large workshops on an upper floor, and the spacious yard at the back had boilers and equipment used for the preparation of food.

The Committee indulged in a good deal of self-justification when the figure for the re-building was announced, saying to justify the expenditure, that it really was an absolutely essential piece of work. The whole thing added up to £5,563 18s 8d, which seems laughable to us nowadays, faced as we have been with a bill for £68,000 for the rebuilding that took place in 1970.

In 1909 the Home had hired two motor and six horse vans from a firm called Tillings. Each van was painted red and had the name of the Home painted in large letters on its sides. Eight new men were engaged to accompany the vans, sitting by the driver and keeping an eye on the dogs they fetched. Seventy-eight police stations in the County of London were to be visited daily by the horse vans, and forty-nine in Outer London by the motor vans. This was a new experiment that was to prove enormously successful, for the Home still runs a similar fleet of vans, only nowadays each motor truck is handled by a single woman, who deals both with the driving and with the dogs.

By 1914 all Europe was living under the shadow of the coming war, a war that was to prove more bloody and more world-involving than any before.

The years before had been years of empire building. Large tracts of unclaimed land in Africa and the Far East had been taken over by European countries, and now the United States and Russia were following a policy of continental expansion.

When all the available land had been claimed and had national flags firmly clamped in the soil, there began to be ominous talk of war, for the powers inevitably began then to covet each other's possessions.

Germany, although she led the world in the field of commerce and military power, felt she had missed out in the rat race for territory, and most particularly she viewed with covetous eyes the size of the ever-expanding British Empire, where young men lacking opportunity in this crowded island could seek their fortunes in the wide open spaces of Australia, Canada, New Zealand and Africa. Germany had no such outlet. She had nothing comparable to offer her pushing young men, and there were many of them. The opportunity they had, in fact, was to die for their Fatherland in the stinking mud of the trenches, for Germany's casualties were about two million.

A third of the Battersea staff volunteered in the early months of the war, and more were to follow. These men went on the specific understanding that they would be reinstated when they returned. Nobody realized in those early days that the cream of young manhood was going to be skimmed off the population of this country during the four years that lay ahead. England was split overnight into two factions; those who went and those who stayed. So it was at Battersea, but evidence of a certain complacency creeps into the reports of the Committee, most of whom must have been too old to join the colours, though there was hardly a family in England that came through the war unscathed.

The Home continued, and perhaps it was the very fact that such institutions carried on as normally as possible that showed the inner strength and morale of the country that eventually was to carry us to victory, albeit on the backs of the American soldiers who arrived in 1917 when our casualty figures were already more than a million.

At the outset of the war there was a temporary falling-off in the number of dogs received, but this was put down to the fact that many people wanted their dogs as companions and guards while their young men were at the front. Many dogs were brought in by their masters who were leaving on active service. After making desperate and fruitless attempts to find homes for their pets, they were obliged to have them destroyed. Some of the scenes of leave-taking in the yard at Battersea were so touching as to rival those taking place at main line stations all over the country.

The clinic that had been run for some years and served a section of the public that otherwise would be unable to afford adequate veterinary treatment for their pets, had to be closed. The veterinary surgeon, John Stow Young, had joined the

Royal Army Veterinary Corps. However, in 1916 the Committee were able to re-open this clinic, and a Mr F. W. Chamberlain held twice-weekly sessions as in the old days.

By then the staff had been decimated, for twenty out of the thirty-six had gone on active service, but the numbers of dogs were soaring once more. One does not get the feeling that the Committee of that time knew exactly what the problems were that faced the Secretary and his dwindling band of men. The Chairman at the Annual General Meeting was to say '... but those were the piping times of peace, while now we are face to face with devastating war – indeed, I think the principal interest in this Report is that it shows how in these times of trouble and anxiety through which we are passing, the Home has been able sucessfully to cope with the situation.' The Committee decided that in future they would endeavour to recruit their staff from ex-Service men, which shows a somewhat unrealistic outlook in view of the overwhelming shortage of manpower that was bound to sweep the country.

Money poured into the coffers of the Home, which found itself on a firmer financial foundation than ever before, but the day to day running of the Home must have been a vast and nightmarish problem for the few remaining staff and the additional elderly men who had been taken on to the strength. It says a lot for the drive and determination of the secretaries, Mr Guillum Scott, and Mr Guy Rowley who succeeded him in 1916, that the Home did in fact go on running, and running smoothly. It puts one in mind of the stately swan that looks so majestic gliding through the water, but nobody thinks of those great webbed feet flipping madly underneath.

It says even more for Rowley and his men that when in 1917 the Home Office authorities suggested that it would become necessary to destroy all dogs left unclaimed at the end of three days, an indignant letter was written from the Dogs' Home pointing out the extreme hardship that such a measure would entail, not only to the general public, but also to the

Home. Perhaps the Dog's Home did, in fact, provide an oasis of sanity in the desert of war, and that war was weathered there, as have been all the other storms that have battered the patch of ground in Battersea that harbours more than eighteen thousand dogs each year.

15
Publicity: the 1920s and 30s

The year 1918 saw not only the end of the war, but it also saw the birth of publicity in this country – the embryonic form of what we see today.

A picture of a small black pekinese from Battersea appeared in the *Daily Mirror,* the caption stating that Princess's days were numbered unless a purchaser could be found for her and touchingly describing her as 'the smallest inmate'. Would-be buyers were told to apply to the Dogs' Home.

Within a matter of hours the office was inundated by more than three thousand enquiries by letter, telegram and telephone from people imploring to be allowed the privilege of buying this little dog. The happy outcome of the incident was that the dog's owner from whom she had been stolen three months earlier recognized her pet, and so they were reunited once again.

The war emergency was over, and people were looking forward to a certain peace and plenty, and they were determined to enjoy themselves come what may. The four years that had gone before had taught them something of the transiency of life. Headlines 'ENGLAND IN PERIL' or CAN WE AVOID DISASTER? no longer meant that a new front was being breached, but merely that our test cricket team was in trouble. Dancing was the main pastime, the 'Twinkle', the 'Jog Trot', the 'Missouri Walk' were followed by the smoother 'Blues', but the 'Blues' was superseded by the jerky 'Charleston' and the 'Black Bottom'. Dining out was becoming fashionable, and where you dined you danced; later you also danced where you drank tea and ate cream cakes.

Dogs from Battersea were constantly hitting the headlines. Lupino Lane, famous acrobat and songster of the twenties, a member of the Lupino family that had been famed as acrobats since 1780, and who achieved his greatest fame with the 'Lambeth Walk' that was to sweep the country in the thirties, came down to the Home. He chose himself a nice bull-terrier. Next day there was a news item headed 'Some people have all the luck'. It carried on:

Look at Lupino Lane. The other day he thought he would buy a bull terrier, so off he went to the Dogs' Home where he is known as a lover of dogs, and secured a handsome bull terrier for 30s. On the way back he thought the animal appeared to be ailing, so he dropped into the vet's, just to be on the safe side. 'I think you have more than one dog,' was the verdict. And the vet was right. For a mere song like 30s Lupino is now the owner of not one but five bull terriers, and all of them apparently thorough-breds.

A terrier from Battersea found herself in central Africa, where, instead of barking at buses, she was able to yap excitedly at the heels of rhinos, and she became the subject of a book. This was a little fox-terrier bought by the big-game hunter and photographer, Cherry Kearton, for the princely sum of 7s 6d. He took the dog on safari with him in Africa, the main object of which was to photograph lions in their natural surroundings.

After a long journey, at last they reached a Masai kraal where they found the villagers in a great state of excitement, for two man-eating lions were known to be in the neighbour-hood. These animals were getting far too bold, and were even allowing themselves to be seen in the day time.

Trackers were sent out and they brought back the news that the lion and his mate were lying under a big thorn-tree only a short distance away. All that remained was for the cameras to be brought up.

The Masai were as excited as Cherry Kearton for no prize

is so keenly coveted among their warriors as the mane of a lion, but to be entitled to wear it as a trophy, a man must have killed the animal single-handed. As the Masai of those days fought with spear and shield alone, those who by their feat of skill and courage wore the lion's mane head-dress had good reason for pride.

The hunters advanced cautiously through the scrub, four Somali horsemen riding out as scouts to try to entice the lions forward, the rest of the party formed in a semi-circular line.

When they were within eighty yards of the tree where the lions were said to be lying, Kearton to his horror found his little dog, Pip, by his side. She had broken loose, determined to join in the fun. This was no joke, and Kearton sternly ordered the dog to stay where she was leaving his camera bearer in charge.

The advance continued until, after fixing the tripod of his camera firmly in the ground, Kearton looked up to see a scene he was never to forget. Step by cautious step, the Masai were advancing, spears poised in the air, while the lions, mad with rage, were tearing at the earth with their forepaws. Then the two great animals began to give vent to their anger with a series of terrifyingly ear-splitting growls and roars. Kearton began to shoot the thrilling scene, but no sooner had his fingers touched the handle of his camera than the lioness sprang out towards a mounted Somali who had ventured a fraction too close. Missing her prey, she bounded off, and was not seen again.

A few seconds later her mate, the lion, made a half-hearted attempt to pounce out, but he evidently was wise enough to realize the strategic strength of his position, surrounded as he was by short and almost impenetrable thorn-bush. Remaining motionless in his lair, he uttered a series of rumbles from the depths of his stomach intended to unnerve the enemy. In Cherry Kearton's case, as he freely admitted, this gambit met with entire success.

Meanwhile, Kearton was not finding the manipulation of his camera any too easy. The bushes which stopped the warriors from reaching their target also impeded his camera work. If it had not been so deadly serious, the situation would have been funny. The Masai were continually changing position, challenging the lion to come out at one moment, and the next casting about for a position from which to launch their spears, and coming between lens and lion each time Kearton thought he was going to get a really good shot.

Excitement was mounting each moment, until, with a swift streak of dull yellow, the lion sprang too swiftly to be intercepted by a spear. He made for a small dried-up river-bed full of thorn-bushes that offered more good cover, and was about eighty yards away.

With a jerk of horror, Kearton realized that the beast must pass within a few yards of his boy, Killenjui and Pip, the dog. However, although the lion paused by them for one sickening moment, it went on to seek the cover of the thorns. There it remained silent, even while being pelted by stones.

The warriors withdrew to consult. Suddenly an idea sprang to Kearton's mind, engendered by the wild excited barks that were issuing from the little dog, all too anxious to join in the battle. Perhaps Pip could be induced to draw out their prey. He had a mental picture of her barking furiously just out of the range of the lion's spring, the lion rising to the bait and leaving its cover to deal with this pest. The Masai would then leap into the breach with their spears to finish off the noble beast.

Pip needed no encouragement to go into the fray, and a moment later they heard the lion's terrifying roar mingled with the excited yapping of the little dog. The plucky little animal had leaped right into the bush and plunged on top of the great tawny beast.

The hunting party broke up in confusion, and for a moment all was pandemonium as they ran hither and thither, not quite knowing how to deal with this new situation. The yapping of the dog suddenly stopped and so did the roaring of the lion. A moment later one of the camera bearers rushed up to Kearton to say that he thought that the lion had killed one of the warriors, but he did not know what had happened to Pip. Nobody seemed to know what had happened to the game little dog.

Going closer, Kearton at once could see the lion lying dead on the ground, and beside him what appeared to be the dead body of the Masai. But there was no sign of the dog. Suddenly the 'corpse' of the warrior sprang to life, and shouting angrily, he held out a bleeding hand.

What had happened was that the plucky little dog from Battersea had dived into the lion's hiding place, and attacked the great animal by seizing its tail. She held on with grim determination, and nothing the lion could do would shake her loose. He could not reach her, nor could he rid himself of her, and so he had his attention entirely taken up with the pest. Silently the Masai warrior had crept up and plunged his spear straight into the beast's heart.

In a fight where two warriors cannot determine who did the actual killing, the much-coveted mane goes to the man who retains hold of the beast's tail. What did this Masai warrior then find when he triumphantly seized the tip of the tail but the growling and ferocious Pip, who was damned if she was going to let go, except just long enough to bite the warrior's hand, before she seized hold of the lion's tail once more, her symbol of success.

So it was that Pip earned herself not only the lion's mane, but also the name of Simba the Lion – that little stray that hailed from the Dog's Home, Battersea, many thousands of miles away, to which we must now return.

It says a lot for the happy relations that always prevailed in the Home to record that not one man came out at either Battersea or at Hackbridge during the General Strike. The men who looked after the railway horses downed tools and left their charges to be looked after by volunteers[1] during the strike which lasted for ten days. 'When the bells rang at midnight on Monday, 3rd May, over the silent cities, they

---

[1] One of these volunteers was the present Chairman of the Dogs' Home, Lord Cottesloe.

announced the beginning of a stillness which nobody had ever known before in English history. . . .' 'There were no trains, no bus services, no trams, no papers, no building, no power', but the keepers at the Dogs' Home still came to work. Some of them had to walk long distances and some of them slept at the kennels, but they came to work and the dogs were fed.

In 1932 there was a gala night at the Piccadilly Hotel, the 'Tail Waggers' Night', in order to raise money to pay for dog licences for those unable to afford the necessary 7s 6d. The Dogs' Home sent six dogs to be put up for auction by Sonny Hale and Jessie Matthews, and by the long arm of coincidence which, as the reporter in the *Bystander* put it, 'if employed by a writer of fiction would earn him the condemnation of all the critics', one of those six dogs turned out to be the lost dog of the head chef at that very hotel.

Another incident of the same kind happened in 1948 when *The Star* held a dog tournament at Wembley which included a demonstration by the guard dogs of the RAF, a dog show in which all breeds were represented, and a homeless dogs' parade with twelve dogs from Battersea, one of which was claimed by someone in the assembled crowd.

To bring themselves in line with contemporary thought and action, the Home became an incorporated society in 1933, and shortly afterwards a staff pension scheme was introduced. The Home at Bow was in operation, though in effect it only acted as a transit hostel, those dogs that were fit enough being transferred to Battersea for sale.

In 1936 a black and white fox-terrier called Spider that belonged to the zoo was lost and found at Battersea. Another black and white gentleman also put in an appearance at the Home. This was a black and white cocker spaniel that had the sagacity to lose itself on the Fulham football ground – club colours, black and white – so on the completion of his week in the Home and remaining unclaimed, he returned to the other side of the river, where he became the mascot of the football club.

Two hundred-weight of bones were found in a cellar under the buildings in the Judges' Triangle at the Law Courts after Nell, a fox-terrier-type bitch, was evicted after living there for nine years. She was taken to the Dogs' Home, and happy to say, she ended her days in comfort with a family in Hendon.

There are many strange coincidences, but one of the strangest must be that of a woman who came to the Home in search of her chow-chow lost the day before in Hyde Park. As she left the Home sorrowfully after a fruitless search, who should come trotting along the pavement jauntily towards her but the missing dog.

Scruffy, the famous dog film-star of the thirties was once a Battersea stray. This clever little dog refused to perform unless he was given a diet of tinned salmon, all other tempting titbits being summarily rejected.

Another amusing story is told of a dog that was bought from the Home by Lord Fingall's son. This was a small Yorkshire terrier that gloried in the name *Larkin*, called after the revolutionary Irish leader. One day the dog strayed again, and after a great hue and cry, was found sitting on a ham in the larder of a Kensington lady. With bared teeth and ferocious growls, the little dog refused to let anyone come near him until his master arrived.

These, of course, are only a very few of the stories that fill the pages of the Press cuttings books at Battersea but they are a few that serve to illustrate the general pattern of life at the Dogs' Home.

16

The Second World War and After

At Battersea the start of this new war to end all wars followed the same pattern as the beginning of that other war that had been destined to end all wars. Within a matter of weeks four members of the Committee and five members of the staff were 'somewhere in England' training for active service. The Bow Home, which had really only proved to be a complete white elephant from the outset, was closed, though a day and a night watchman had to be maintained. A representative of the Dogs' Home was sent to sit on a special committee that was hurriedly set up and called the National ARP Animals' Committee.

The threat of fire was uppermost in the mind of the secretary at that time, Mr Healey-Tutt, and he himself elected to sleep in the paint-shed and act as a fire guard. He took his duties and responsibilities so much to heart that eventually he had to be given indefinite leave of absence to recover his health. Ten years later he was to develop Parkinson's Disease, and he retired in 1954 and went to live with his daughter in South Africa.

By mid-September 1940, London was fully to understand what Winston Churchill had meant when he had offered nothing but 'blood, toil, tears, and sweat'. The Battle of Britain was at its climax, and during the months of August and September 1,244 German aircraft were destroyed.

Although an ever-increasing number of people were arriving at the Home bringing with them their pets and asking for them to be destroyed, Mr Healey-Tutt showed great wisdom. He told this stream of distraught dog-owners not to be in too much of a hurry but to bide their time and see what happened. It was the fear of the unknown more than anything else that drove people to extreme actions of this kind, the same sort of fear that had sent the floods of refugees crowding on to the roads of France in the early days of the war. Healey-Tutt did not want people to live to regret an action that had been taken at a moment of panic. His job, he was sure, was to save the lives of dogs: not to take them unnecessarily.

That was a nightmare winter. The uneven drone of the German bombers followed closely night after night on the unearthly wailing rise and fall of the sirens, and then came the blasting and the terror. Yet somehow London survived, and with it the Dogs' Home. There was a direct hit in the drive, but providentially it fell exactly midway between the main gates and the Whittington Lodge. Although there was a great deal of damage, there was no loss of life.

Incendiary bombs fell in droves into the kennels, but as they came through the skylights that ran in a straight line along the centre of the roofs, they therefore fell in the passage running below the pens, mercifully causing little damage. There was a constant fire guard maintained, and temporary repairs were always put in hand within a few days. At no time was the work of the Home interrupted, but the moment one repair had been finished, then there came another raid, more blasting, more incendiaries, more damage . . . and so it went over and over again.

Still the dogs were brought in; some were claimed, some went to new homes, and those that were left were painlessly destroyed. Life at Battersea went on as usual.

On 16 April 1941 a land-mine fell on one of the gasometers right behind the exercising grounds. This could easily have been the end of the Home – and of half of Battersea – but although there was considerable damage from the blast to woodwork and windows, the extraordinary thing is that

114

there was really very little harm done. It was as if the place was charmed, and it is fantastic when one views the Home's close proximity to the Battersea power station, the gasometers and the railways that run down two sides, to relate that there was not one casualty to man or beast during the whole of the war.

It was in that same year, 1941, that a heart-rending order had to be carried out. A return had to be made to the old three-day stay at the Home before the dogs were disposed of. This measure was the result mainly of the desperate food shortage, this in itself accounting for the enormous numbers of dogs that were being admitted to the Home. Too many people lacked the courage to bring their animals to the Home to be destroyed when the time came when they could be kept no longer. These people took the coward's way out, and turned their animals out into the streets where they would either starve or be killed by a bomb. However, a close examination of the records shows that to a large extent this three-day ruling was ignored, or perhaps a Nelsonian blind eye was turned, for quite seventy-five per cent of the dogs were kept for at least six days.

By the middle of the war more and more members of the staff were being called up, and the pattern of the First World War was being played out again. The Battersea dogs were not left out of the war effort, for seven airedales and seven alsations were recruited by an enterprising RAF commandant to be trained as sentries at his station. An allowance of two-pence a day for meat was obtained – about the equivalent of the ration allowed for human consumption at that time – and no doubt the dogs did very well at the NAAFI when they were not guarding the entrances to the camp.

During the war, British dogs were trained to guard vital points against air-borne attack, to track down parachutists, to undertake liaison work and to lay wires across country under such concentrated fire that a man could not hope to carry out the work. They were trained as ammunition carriers, Red Cross workers and as canine mine detectors.

The Germans took a very different view of the dog's duties in war-time from that taken by the British authorities. They entered the war in 1939 with 50,000 highly trained animals that had been subjected to rigorous German discipline – there was no room for sentiment there – and these defenceless animals were dropped by parachute to seek out and explode landmines when the mechanical mine detectors were defeated owing to the mines being housed in wooden or plastic cases. German dogs were trained to hurl themselves under tanks, blowing them up with the bombs attached to their backs. It is difficult to imagine what would be the response to such an order in the British Army.

Back at Battersea, only the older staff now remained, and a very limited number of new men. All of them were called upon to work long hours, and in addition, there were the firewatching duties too. This was the general picture everywhere in the country – there was no room for shirkers – and it is no surprise to learn that the kennels at Battersea were always kept spotlessly clean, and pre-war standards prevailed as far as was humanly possible. Maintenance was the only thing that suffered badly, for any material available had quickly to be used for bomb damage repair and, needless to say, all building supplies were so scarce as to be almost non-existent.

Problems did in fact arise over the arrangement of suitable firefighting facilities. Healey-Tutt, overburdened and overwrought, left to carry far more responsibility than he was able, became desperately worried at the idea of having to make a reciprocal arrangement with another body of firefighters. He feared that any strangers being called in to the Home might have great difficulty in handling panic-stricken dogs, and did not like the idea of his own men being absent, called out to help elsewhere. The authorities were not sympathetic, they had far too many more pressing problems, and they merely curtly pointed out that unless the Home was prepared to help others, it could not expect to get help itself.

That Healey-Tutt was left to carry the can becomes increasingly obvious. The Committee simply were not aware of the overwhelming difficulties facing this man, keenly anxious to keep things as normal as possible. Staff was desperately short, and food almost unobtainable, though Healey-Tutt very sensibly took the precaution of doing a certain amount of stock-piling, an act that was unofficially condoned by the authorities. Petrol was strictly rationed, and when the poor man went to ask, not to have his petrol supply increased, but just maintained at the same level, he was rudely told that the best way of dealing with the problem of the stray dogs would be to have gas chambers at all the police stations. The unwanted animals could then be destroyed on the spot.

Healey-Tutt had always had extremely good relations with the police, and this fact was to stand him and the Home in very good stead. His contacts at Scotland Yard proved a tower of strength to him, and he was able to go to them not only for the wise advice that they gave him freely, but also to arrange a certain amount of the adroit string-pulling that went on behind the scenes, not only over the maintenance of petrol supplies, but also over food. Through the kind offices of the Commissioner of Metropolitan Police, the Dogs' Home drivers were eventually listed during the last year of the war under the Essential Works Order, as it was found that the older men who had to be employed simply could not manage the work.

Ten days after the cessation of hostilities on the Western Front, the order went out that the dogs could be kept for seven days once more. Although this order raised many problems in view of the acute shortage of food, it did mean that the war was to all intents and purposes over. Once more the Dogs' Home had bridged a crisis, and came through, colours flying and virtually unscathed.

The end of the war was the end of an epoch for the Dogs' Home. The early struggles and crises were over, and what has followed has been the day to day running of the Home, with its attendant small dramas, both amusing and touching.

In 1945 after the war was over, the Duke of Beaufort, who had consented to become President of the Home on the death of the Duke of Portland in 1943, paid his first visit to Battersea.

The Home has always been extremely fortunate in its presidents. There have only been four in all. First there was the Marquess of Townshend, noted as an animal-lover *par excellence,* who took the chair at the first historic meeting, and was President for more than twenty years. He was succeeded by the Earl of Onslow, who resigned in 1887 on learning that he was to go to New Zealand as Governor-General in 1889.

The next President was the Duke of Portland, who was to hold this office for fifty-five years. It would seem that the offices of President of the Dogs' Home, Battersea and that of Master of the Horse are a dual role, for the Duke of Portland was Master of the Horse from 1886-92 and again from 1895-1905. The Duke of Beaufort, President of the Home since 1943, has been Master of the Horse since 1936.

When the Duke of Beaufort wrote to accept the invitation to become President of the Home, he said, 'Although I shall not be able to take a very active part, I hope to attend the Annual Meeting and pay occasional visits to the Home.' That was nearly thirty years ago, and since then he has paid repeated visits to the Home, and has won a firm place in the affections of all connected with it. His tireless interest and concern in the Home and with its activities have always been shared by the Duchess of Beaufort.

Some years ago they showed their practical interest by taking a dog from the Home whose master was serving a sentence of five years at Dartmoor. This dog, Bobo, was made welcome at Badminton, and very soon she and the Duke were inseparable. Where the master was, Bobo was sure to be found. When the time for Bobo's original owner to come out of gaol, the Duchess, who had written to him during the five years, arranged for Bobo to stay with them at Badminton (where she eventually died) as she was so happy there. Bobo has now been replaced, though never in the affections of her owners, by a pekinese, Pity Me, and a pretty, though perhaps as the Duke says, a trifle too fox-like, mongrel. Together these two Battersea strays rule the ducal house with velvet paws.

The story of the years since the war is like a shower of rain, composed of single drops, each one being a story ranging from the pathetic to the banal, from the funny to the sad, some stories with happy endings, but many, many more without. Not all dogs end up in ducal homes – not all dogs end up in a home at all. The only home they will know is the one at Battersea, which will be their last.

This book would never have been written had it not been for the laborious research undertaken by one of the ex-keepers, Mr Jack Tyler, who still works at the Home as a clerk. Mr Tyler started as a keeper quite by chance in 1934 when he came out of the Army and was looking for a job. He happened to go into the Labour Exchange one morning, only to be told that there was nothing for him. 'Where are all those men going, then?' he asked, pointing to a group of men crowding up the stairs. 'Oh, they are going to apply for the job of keeper at the Dogs' Home,' was the answer. Jack Tyler was quick to act, and that afternoon he was first in the queue for an interview with Mr Healey-Tutt. They talked for an hour about East Africa where they had both served and, needless to say, Tyler got the job.

Mr Tyler offers the following prescription for success as a keeper at the Dogs' Home:

1 The qualities of a saint, combined with an ability to tell a white lie at times, and to sum people up in an instant, plus an excellent memory, tact, initiative, and above all, infinite patience.
2 It must be possible to anticipate what a person is about to say. Never tell the public too much, until you are certain that they are genuine. Never make a long story of something that can be told in a few words. Never air your own views, unless you are sure of your facts.
3 Remember that the Home is really run on the same basis as a shop, where there is a well-known saying that 'the customer

is always right'. In this shop the customer is very often wrong, but he must not be told so.

4   If you are bitten by a dog—or customer, for that matter—do not worry, for the Battersea General Hospital is nearby, the service excellent and free. Take care that if you get into an argument with a dog, or a customer, that it is not a big dog— or customer!

5   Remember that dogs are akin to women: it is almost impossible to assess their age beyond the puppy stage. One keeper of long standing was ten years out when judging the age of a bitch (Mr Tyler does not enlighten us as to whether this was dog or customer).

6   These instructions are confined to keepers only. To become a superintendent is really like trying to attain the position of First Lord of the Admiralty or Chancellor of the Exchequer, and there is more, much more, to be absorbed.

All through its long and varied history, the Home seems to have attracted men of outstanding character and ability not only to serve on its staff, but to help the Home in many other ways. The Committee has always had a quota of business men and barristers, and has seldom encouraged people of sentimental turn of mind, even in the early days. The staff, many of whom have been in the Services, carry out their duties with military precision and, since 1954, when Mr Healey-Tutt went to South Africa, a retired naval Lieutenant-Commander, Benjamin Knight, has been at the helm, running the place with a brisk quarter-deck efficiency.

However, it is not all spit and polish. The keepers and kennelmen handle their charges with gentleness and firm affection, and although they cannot afford to make favourites, it is inevitable that some dogs are more lovable than others. Is not this also true of humans?

17

Your Battersea Dog

The dog that you take home with you from Battersea is no ordinary dog. He is a dog with a problem, and you will have a specific job to do, building up his confidence and making sure that he has a chance to become a happy member of your household.

Nobody knows what has happened to this dog. Nobody knows what he has been through, what bitter experiences may have warped his doggy mind. You do not have a pedigree that you can study, nor even parents you can see to help you to judge how your dog is likely to turn out. There is nobody on whom you can pin the blame if your dog develops tiresome habits. When you adopt a child, something is generally known about its antecedents, but when you adopt a dog from Battersea, you are taking it blind. Its past may be a closed book, but its future lies in your hands.

All dogs crave for and need human affection, but your stray dog is going to want a double share. You will have to make much of him and try to create for him a pattern of life into which he will fit, and in which he is going to feel happy and secure. You must give him a comfortable framework of regular hours from the start. He must know right from the beginning that he can count on being taken for a daily walk and that his food will arrive at the expected time.

When you first take him home, remember that he has had a trying time, and he will need to be very quiet for a few days to help him to get over all that has happened to him during the last week or two. Those anxious days of waiting, nose pressed to the bars of his pen, hoping against hope that his master will come to claim him. That agonized howling when a figure appears round the corner, and the strangeness of the surroundings with all the battery of noise and comings and goings.

Veterinary Care

If you do not already have a veterinary surgeon, then ask your friends who have dogs to give you a name. Ask the vet to call and see your dog if possible. It is worth the additional cost if this initial examination can be done in the privacy of your own home and not after a long wait in a crowded surgery. The vet will probably prefer it. This veterinary inspection is most important, as it is possible that your dog could be harbouring an infection which, caught in the early stages, could be dealt with quite easily, but if left, could develop into something really serious. Your veterinary surgeon will probably advise you to let him give the dog a series of injections to protect it from the triple enemies of hard-pad, distemper and contagious hepatitis. Be guided by his advice.

Dogs are like people – they are all different. They cannot therefore be treated alike, as their reactions will differ in a given set of circumstances. The puppy that has been dropped into the river with a stone round its neck is going to take a dim view of being encouraged to have a swim. The dog that has been flung out of a car on a crowded motorway is likely to be afraid of traffic for the rest of its life. The dog that has been a habitual wanderer is going to present you with a different problem from the one that has lived a sheltered life and has only landed up at the Dogs' Home on the death of its owner perhaps, by an accident or by sheer chance.

You are going to need a great deal of patience, for it is imperative that you gain the confidence of your Battersea dog, and having once gained that confidence, you must take care never to do anything that will undermine your relationship with the animal.

Your Battersea Dog

Introduction

When you bring your dog home, be very careful when introducing him to the family. Do it quietly, and do not let the children fall on him with enraptured cries. If he is inclined to be timid or nervous he may react by snapping, and that would be a bad start. Let them come quietly, one by one. Limit his new acquaintances to those in the immediate family circle at first. The time for your friends to come and admire your new dog will be when he has settled down and knows his way around. Make sure, however, that they too, approach him quietly and allow him to smell or lick the back of their hands before they attempt to handle him. If he shows any nervousness or signs of temper, leave him alone for the time being. The chances are that after a few weeks, or even days, when he really feels at home, he will become friendly and outgoing of his own accord. To force him in the early stages may be disastrous.

It is highly unlikely that the keepers at Battersea will have allowed you to bring away a dog that is naturally vicious – they develop an uncannily shrewd eye and an instinct for the right sort of dog over the years. And not only the right sort of dog, but also the right sort of owner. Kenneth Hare-Scott writing in *Everybody's Weekly* in 1949 shrewdly observed:

> Had I seemed undesirable to the Keeper with long practice, he would have been unable to discover any dog suitable for me. If necessary he would have pronounced them all in turn as dead, dying or vicious.

It would be just as well not only to limit his new human friends for the first week or two, but to keep him isolated from other dogs. It must be repeated that a clean bill of health from the Dogs' Home does not mean that your dog may not be harbouring a disease that takes longer than a week to incubate, and would therefore be impossible for the Dogs' Home veterinary surgeon to diagnose before the dog was taken away.

Name this dog

You will have to give your new dog a name, but remember that his original name may have been anything from Montmorency to Sam, so choose something short that will be easy for him to learn. Choose something, too, that will **not make** you feel foolish when you are calling him to heel. Some names, while seeming appropriate, when called aloud can make one feel remarkably silly – try calling 'Droopy' several times. Remember too that all dogs start off by being small, and a cross-bred labrador-alsatian that is a little woolly bundle at ten weeks old, is going to sound a bit silly when full-grown if he is called Tiny.

Handling

Do not pick your dog up more than you have to; and when you do have to, make sure that you do it gently but firmly. Rough handling can easily change a good-tempered dog into a snappy or nervous one. Lift him, if he is small enough, by placing one hand under his buttocks and the other under his neck, thus supporting his hindquarters on your forearm and elbow. This is particularly important in the case of a puppy, who should never be held up under his elbows, the rest of him dangling down.

Living Quarters

Give your new dog his own special place in your home. The average dog is a cheery extrovert, and asks for nothing better than to join you in hearth and home. Even so, he likes to have a place that is his exclusively and does not have to be shared. The important thing is that whatever you choose should be large enough for the dog to be able to lie stretched out, and to turn around without being cramped. This goes for a beautiful basket from an expensive shop or just a piece of rug or an old cardboard box. It should be easily cleaned and draught-proof. Dogs are like humans in that they hate draughts and damp, so do what you can to protect him and keep him in good health and condition. Small dogs like a cushion, and provided this is covered with a rug or towel, it will do excellently. Chairs are really for human beings and not for dogs, so the sooner he learns this basic lesson, the better from every point of view. Beds are the same, only more so.

Feeding

Give your dog his own feeding dish and water bowl, making sure the latter is washed and refilled daily, and readily available.

Dogs are like babies in that they attract a lot of well-meant but often ill-conceived advice. It is better, where feeding is concerned, to follow the dictates of your own common sense and find out what suits your dog best. Some dogs readily digest and thrive on raw meat to which has been added a proportion of starchy food – brown bread, biscuits, etc., but others do best on cooked meat. The keepers at the Home will give you good advice on how much you should give your dog daily, which will of course vary according to his size. A rough guide is that he should have as much as he can eat in ten minutes, or two thirds of an ounce of food per pound of the dog's body weight each day, i.e., a dog that weighs 15 lbs will thus have 10 ozs of food – it is as simple as that. A bitch in whelp is obviously going to need more, as is a working dog. Remember that the dog will get bored if he has the same old thing day after day, so try to vary his diet as much as you can, giving him fish occasionally, and a change either in the type of meat you offer him, or in the proprietary tins, which all vary. If using tinned food, choose the ones that state clearly what they contain.

The keepers will have given you a rough idea of your dog's age. If he is still under a year old, it would be as well to start him with three small meals a day, letting him graduate after a few months to one large one in the early evening. The advantage of giving the main meal in the evening is that he will more easily be able to digest and assimilate it at that time of day, because he is likely to rest for a longer time than during any other part of the twenty-four hours.

Dogs, while needing to have clean water available, also

thrive on milk, so do not worry if your new pet drinks the cat's milk. The cat will be the only sufferer.

Bones are good for dogs, though a few dogs cannot digest them. Give him a large cooked mutton bone regularly – but never cooked chicken or rabbit bones, which are liable to splinter and damage the dog's stomach. A large cooked bone will help to keep his teeth clean and to increase the flow of saliva, thus aiding the digestion of the starchy part of his food.

Exercise

Your dog must have exercise if he is going to keep healthy, and exercise means regular walks with you – not having the front door opened for him and being shooed out to go off by himself. If you do that, in all probability you will never see him again, as he may not be lucky enough to end up at the Dogs' Home a second time.

A sharp run will often act as a mild and natural aperient, and the effect of regular exercise, and more particularly the lack of it, is soon apparent in the condition of a dog's skin and coat.

Grooming

Buy a suitable brush and comb for your dog and use them regularly, though avoid tugging at a tangled matted coat. Approach your dog with caution at first when grooming him, as here he may have had some bad experiences in the past.

When choosing the grooming tools, bear in mind both the sensitivity of his skin and also the texture of his coat. Obviously, what will do for a whippet will not do for a poodle or a sheepdog, i.e., a short-coated fine-skinned dog needs a softer and shorter-bristled brush than one that would be used for a dog with a dense, harsh and curly coat.

Your dog will also be in need of a regular bath, especially if you live in a big city. This again should be approached with caution, and it is better to use the brush and comb with a dry shampoo and give the bath a miss if there is any chance either of the dog being frightened or of his lying round with a wet coat for any length of time. A good dog shampoo should be used, and great care must be taken to see that all the soap is rinsed out of his coat. A spray is the ideal instrument for the purpose. Let all the water run away before you attempt to take the dog out of bath or sink or you will find that the dog is not the only person having a bath. A large, old towel spread on the floor in which to envelop him as soon as he comes out will catch a lot of the drips, and prevent him from shaking himself all over you.

Mouth
Check his teeth from time to time, and take professional advice if you have any doubts. Some dogs quite enjoy having their teeth cleaned with a small toothbrush, but you can achieve the same effect with a piece of cotton wool soaked in an ordinary mouth-wash or peroxide of hydrogen (ten volumes per cent) diluted with three or four parts of tepid water. Remember that your dog's tongue, gums, lips and cheeks are highly sensitive. You will need to show great patience when you are performing this task.

Eyes and Ears
Keep your dog's eyes clean by wiping them when necessary with a piece of cotton wool. Clean the ears by wiping the insides and flaps with a soft flannel or sponge wrung out in warm soapy water. Any sign of irritation is a signal to take him to see the veterinary surgeon. Do not attempt to treat ear conditions yourself, and on no account poke about in the ear with cotton wool on the end of an orange-stick.

Feet
His toe-nails should be examined regularly to make sure that they are not growing too long or that one nail is not growing out of proportion to the rest. You will find that regular pavement exercise will help to wear the nails down evenly. If you cut your dog's nails yourself, use a pair of cutters or clippers, and take very great care not to cut them too near to the quick. Examine his dew claws – the ones on the inside of his forelegs – from time to time, as they can get torn and damaged.

Training

Now for his training. Bear in mind the fact that he may or may not have had some training in his previous existence, but you should be able to tell fairly accurately just how much when you have had him for a few days. Nothing is worse than a spoilt dog, and it is easier to spoil a dog than it is to spoil a child. The spoilt child will have the benefit of facing up to the rough and tumble of school. Your dog will not be so fortunate.

Nowadays there are excellent dog-training classes held in most big towns, and very often clubs have been started in the country too. It would be quite a good idea to enrol at one of these and take him along once a week, but first I must break a piece of news to you. At these classes, it will not so much be the dog that is being trained, as you yourself. He will not know this, though, and if he did, he would not hold it against you.

The first piece of training for your Battersea dog will be to teach him his name. Take him somewhere where you will be entirely alone with him and where he will be quite safe and devote half an hour to familiarizing him with this new name. Make much of him, and at the same time call him by his name. Let him wander about, and then call him back by his name again. If he responds quickly, give him a reward. This does not come under the heading of bribery at this stage. It is called 'getting the dog's confidence'. Later on you will find a pat or a rub over his head will be enough.

The next important thing is to find out how far he has got with his house training. He may be all right in this respect, but if not, then you must take great care to instil good habits. Watch him carefully, and at any sign of his asking to go out, see that he can do so immediately. If he does have an accident, scold him gently and take him out straight away. At no time during his re-training must this dog of yours be seriously punished. Sparing the rod may spoil the child, but I can assure you that the use of it will spoil this dog from Battersea.

When you take him out, keep him on the lead all the time at first until you are absolutely certain that he will come to you when called. This may mean that you will have to enrol a willing helper to hold him on a long rope while you stand some way off and call him. Your obedience classes will help you over this, and he will learn the three cardinal orders; 'heel', 'sit' and 'stay'.

He will have to be taught to use the gutter to relieve himself, though I myself have mixed feelings about this, as there is always the danger of a car coming very close. If possible, teach him to wait until he is on grass. Never teach a puppy to use newspaper. Wet, soggy newsprint is impossible to read!

He must be checked if he jumps up. A knee lifted quickly may discourage him, but if he is really bad you must put him down firmly every time he tries to jump up, holding him down and saying 'no'.

Your dog will also have to learn to be left alone without kicking up an infernal din. If he is a puppy, you will have to go out of the door, shutting it behind you. You must resist the temptation to go back as his agonized howls rend the air. This will only give him the idea that he just has to make enough noise for you to reappear. With a grown-up dog, you probably will have to return and tell him to be quiet. It is better, of course, not to leave a dog alone for too long, and I am sure there is no need for me to issue a warning about leaving a dog alone in a car with the windows tightly closed and the sun blazing on it.

Your dog may already be accustomed to travelling in a car, but if not, he must be taught that he has his place, and he must stay in it. Preferably, this is in the very back of the car, or at any rate on the back seat. Dogs that travel on the floor are liable to be car-sick. If your dog shows signs of sickness, remember that it is possible to buy anti-car-sick pills nowadays which are useful on long journeys.

This chapter cannot possibly cover all the queries you may have about the care of your new dog, so if you have any worries, buy yourself a good dog manual, which, even if you do not follow it slavishly, will offer you good advice, and will support you when you have doubts.

18

A Brief Note on the Care of a Cat

The care of a cat is instinctive to a cat-lover, but even so, there are still a few do's and don'ts.

Do not undertake the ownership of a cat unless you are prepared either to keep it in all the time, with all the attendant problems of litter-trays and clawing of furniture, or you can readily accept the fact that a cat must have its freedom. The giving of this freedom does mean that it is possible that one day your cat may not come back, as it may either have wandered away or it may have been the victim of a road accident – it is likely that you will never know its fate.

Do not expect your cat to sit like the cat on the chocolate-box, beribboned, with paws folded and a look of complacency on its rounded features. Cats are not like that. They are demanding creatures, not easily to be brushed aside. If ignored, they have a nasty habit of getting their own back by bringing up their last meal on the drawing-room carpet at the feet of your cat-hating guests.

There is no need to fuss a cat unduly, but it does need attention, preferably undivided at times, and plenty of affection. It needs meals at regular times, a place to call its own, and ample opportunity to get out and about. A cat that is left on its own all day can be very lonely. The perfect solution is to let a female cat have one lot of kittens, keeping one of them, before having her spayed, or to take two toms from the same litter and have them neutered. The two animals will then be company for each other, and their antics as they play will cause you much entertainment and delight.

Do not make the mistake of thinking that your cat will not become very attached to you. It will; and there are even one-man cats, in the same way that there are one-man dogs.

Follow the same principles with your Battersea cat as those outlined in the last chapter with regard to a dog. If you do not already know of a veterinary surgeon, then find one. Have your cat checked over by him at home, and ask him to inject the cat against infectious feline enteritis. Keep the animal strictly isolated for at least seven days.

Treat your Battersea cat very gently. If it shows any signs of being frightened, keep it in one room, taking care that there is no unguarded fire or chimney, and provide it with a litter-tray – an old meat-tray will do, or a plastic washing-up bowl; there are plenty of proprietary cat litters. See that there is fresh water and milk always available and give your cat two or three small meals a day at first. Be prepared to devote a part of the day to giving it fuss and attention, and while you do this, you can also examine its coat and brush and comb it. If your cat does not want to be handled, wait until it makes advances to you of its own accord. Most cats are friendly creatures and, like the rest of us, want to be loved.

Be very careful when introducing the cat to a dog. The chances are that the cat will ignore the dog, but do not risk an accident with your dog's all-too-vulnerable eyes.

Cats are carnivorous animals and therefore they need meat as well as fish. They appear to thrive on the proprietary tinned cat foods; though, like all other animals, they appreciate variety in their diet. There is no need to feed a cat on halibut and minced topside.

It is a fallacy to think that cats can digest bones from cooked poultry. In the wild state, the cat eats what it catches raw, and then the bones dissolve, but this is not so when they have been cooked.

It is terrible to see chairs ravaged by the sharp claws of

cats, and it is absolutely unnecessary. Every time the cat starts plucking at the upholstery say 'No' firmly, and take it away to its scratching post. If the cat does not go outside and use a handy tree, pet shops sell the next best thing.

Follow the same procedure with the grooming of a cat as you would with a dog, especially with the long-haired varieties. Short-haired cats rarely need to be brushed, however, but a long-haired cat will enjoy a daily grooming session, provided there are no tangles in the coat that will pull on its skin.

The ears should be inspected regularly, and if dirty, they can be wiped gently with a piece of cotton-wool that has been dipped in milk of magnesia. As with the dog, any sign of ear trouble should be referred to a vet. The eyes can be bathed with a mild solution of boracic acid powder should there be a slight discharge. Anything more should be dealt with professionally.

Never attempt to trim a cat's claws yourself.

Although they are reputed to have nine lives, this is a legend that has grown up owing to their expertise in getting themselves out of awkward situations that would prove fatal to other animals – possibly the very reason why your Battersea cat survived to come to you. Even so, they do not always fall on their feet, and many have died as a result of falling out of an open window. Curiosity too often is their downfall, and it is all too easy to shut a cat in a cupboard or refrigerator, with fatal results.

Your cat should live for about twelve to fourteen years – I myself have known a cat reach twenty-five – and you will build up a happy and loving relationship over the years. The most important thing to remember with a cat is that it is a thoroughly enjoyable animal, and must not be thought of as part of the furniture.

19

What Lies Ahead

This then is the end of the first century at Battersea. A lot of ground has been covered, and the question we must ask ourselves is what lies ahead? What are the prospects to which we can look forward?

Altogether the outlook is encouraging. Hitherto, in spite of great generosity of supporters by gifts and legacies, finances have prevented a devoted staff from giving the dogs the fullest measure of care and after-care. Disease, initially brought in by many of the dogs that come to the Home, has been spread by cross-infection due to the inevitably crowded conditions. It has not been possible to restore to health many dogs that might have been recoverable, or to keep them for long enough to find them new homes.

The greater part of the kennels have now been rebuilt on the most modern lines, and proposals are outlined to rebuild the rest. The immediate effect of this initial rebuilding has been to reduce disease dramatically. The Home is now selling most of the puppies either taken in or born on the premises, whereas hitherto their chances of survival were infinitesimal.

A new contract has now been drawn up with the police under which the Home will continue to carry out for them their statutory duty of keeping all stray dogs for a week, to enable their owners to claim them. However, the new contract has been based on realistic financial terms in view of the cost of running such a home. This revolutionizes the picture of the Home's financial situation, and the legacies and gifts, while needed more than ever with an expanding programme in view, can now be fully used for their proper purpose: the care and the after-care of the dogs placed in the charge of the Home.

The Committee is embarking on an extensive programme of other improvements.

First and foremost, the conditions for the staff are being brought into line with the standards prevailing nowadays. The Dogs' Home has always been served devotedly by its staff, and their welfare and comfort must have high priority on the list of things to be done.

Secondly, a full veterinary service needs to be provided in place of the two free clinics a week that are all that have hitherto been possible. This does not mean to say that the Home has not always had a first-class veterinary surgeon on call, for it has. What it does mean is that a full-time veterinary surgeon must be provided for in the sole employment of the Dogs' Home.

Thirdly, as said earlier, plans have already been put in train for the rebuilding of the remainder of the kennels at Battersea, thus increasing the capacity so that more dogs can be maintained. This extra accommodation will become increasingly necessary, for with a reduction in the incidence of disease, so the number of dogs in the Home at any one time will swell; and this prospect must be allowed for in the plans.

When this trio of corner-stones have been laid, then an organization will have to be established for the finding of good homes for the much greater number of dogs that will be available for sale.

And this will not be the end, for in the rosy distance of the future can be seen the establishment of another 'Hackbridge', a place that this time will not be destined to provide only for the dogs of the rich, but will truly be a convalescent home for the longer-stay 'patients'.

This is a very full programme that has been outlined, and it is one that will keep the Committee busy for a good many years to come, but it is one they are determined to carry through; and no doubt when all this has been achieved, there will still be plenty more to work on for the future.

The vision of the future is that Battersea should act as a reception centre and clinic where people can come during the first seven days to look for their lost pets. Any dogs that remain unclaimed and which are not sold within a few days because of ill health, can then be taken to a country home which will be manned by a qualified veterinary surgeon who will be assisted by a staff of veterinary nurses and kennelmen or maids. There the dogs will be nursed back to health, and put on sale when they are in good condition.

The most important thing is that everything possible should be done to increase public awareness and understanding, and this in turn will lead to fewer abandoned dogs and less disease, but always with fuller and better care for those that are in the care of the Dogs' Home.

The public must have their eyes fully opened to the fact that pet animals are not toys, but responsibilities not to be lightly undertaken. It must be remembered that once taken on, they are yours for the rest of their all-too-short lives, but you will be buying a lifetime of love and devotion.

Index

Index

Index

Paggen, Peter 27
Parkinson, Mr 21
Parr, Lt Col 79
Parrots taken in at Battersea 64
Pasteur, Louis, vaccine against rabies
60–1; cat lover 69
Pavitt, James 10, 35, 36
Pavitt, Rosa 10
Payne and Clark, architects 22
Peace, Charlie, and his dog 56
Peacock, P. R. 44
Peel, Sir Robert 98
Pigeons taken in at Battersea 64
Ponsonby, Sir Henry 48–9, 50, 74, 75
Portland, Duke of 79, 80, 118
Price's Patent Candle Company 31–2
Pritchard, Professor 79
Prussic acid used to destroy animals 10,
71

Quarantine kennels 81, 85

Rabbits taken in at Battersea 64
Rabies 58–63; dumb rabies 59
Rabies scare in 1880s 52–7, 71
Raynham, Lord, (later Marquess of
Townshend q.v.) 6
Richardson, Benjamin Ward 72
Richardson, Bertram 75
Riffel, Lloyd George's St Bernard 82–4
Roosevelt, Theodore, cat lover 69
Rowley, Guy 104
Royal Free Hospital asks for dogs for
vivisection 42
Royal Society for Prevention of Cruelty
to Animals 6, 32, 42, 43; policy on
vivisection 45

Schneider, Carl, describes his visit to
Dogs' Home 37–8
Schweitzer, Albert, cat lover 69
Scoborio, Mr 47
Scott, Sir Giles Gilbert 32
Scott, Guillum 85, 104
Scott, Robert Falcon 90
Scott, Sir Walter 56
Scruffy, dog film-star 112
Selby, Henry 76
Semple phenolized fixed vaccine 61
Sewell, A. J. 81, 86
Shackleton, Sir Ernest 82, 86, 88–97
Smithells, R. W. 44

Southampton Street receiving house for
dogs 18
Southey, Robert, cat lover 69
Spratts Ltd 81, 86, 87
Star dog tournament at Wembley,
1948 111

Tagg, George 10
'Tail Waggers' night at Piccadilly
Hotel 111
Tealby, Mary 4, 5, 9; enlists support
for dogs' home 6, 16; on committee
8, dies 18
Townshend, Marquess of 118
Tully, Mr, builder of original Battersea
Dogs' Home 22
Two Dog-Shows (article in *All the Year
Round*) 11–16
Tyler, Jack 94, 119; prescription for
success as a keeper 119–20

Victoria, Queen 27; asks private secretary to visit and report on Dogs'
Home 48; adds her name to list of
subscribers 49; Patron of RSPCA
50; Patron of Dogs' Home 50, 51;
concern on dogs' length of stay in
home before being destroyed 49,
50–1; opposition to cremation of dogs
74–5
Vivisection 41–6, 62; justification for
controlled 43–4; anaesthesia used in
44–5; RSPCA policy on 45; dog-
stealing for 101

Wallington Kennels 87
Walpole, Horace, cat lover 69
Ward, Edith 76
Ward, Henry 80, 81
Warren, Sir Charles 54, 55; open letter
to 55–7
Warriner, Mr 21
Watson, William 31
Wellington, 1st Duke of 98
Whittington, Dick 68
Whittington Lodge 64, 70, 71, 114
Wilberforce, William 32
Wild, Frank 96
Williams-Ellis, Clough, designs new
buildings for Dogs' Home 101
Wren, Sir Christopher 27
Wyndoe, George 94

Young, John Stow 85, 86, 87, 103

138